Shakespeare Shorts

Performing Arts

MW01120234

Grades 4-6

Written by David McAleese
Illustrated by David McAleese

ISBN 1-55035-848-0
Copyright 2005
All Rights Reserved * Printed in Canada

Published in the United States by:
On the Mark Press
3909 Witmer Road PMB 175
Niagara Falls, New York
14305
www.onthemarkpress.com

Published in Canada by:
S&S Learning Materials
15 Dairy Avenue
Napanee, Ontario
K7R 1M4
www.sslearning.com

At  Glance™

Learning Expectations	The Plays	Writing Activities	Reading Comprehension Check	Shakespeare Festival Follow-up
Understanding Concepts				
• Describe the characteristics of a tragedy, comedy and historical play	•		•	
• Interpret the meaning of stories and plays	•	•		
• Communicate understanding of plays and stories	•	•		
• Use a variety of drama devices (i.e., mime, tableau)	•			
• Rehearse and present a play	•			
• Interpret a character through gesture, tone of voice, etc.	•			
Critical Analysis & Appreciation				
• Describe story elements (i.e., character, setting, etc.)	•	•	•	
• State interpretation of a play, using proof from the story	•			
• Retell a story in own words	•	•		
• Identify the motivation of a character	•	•	•	
• Identify conflict and resolution in a story	•	•	•	
• Evaluate the performance of a play and give opinions		•		•
• State and support preference for a particular play		•		•
Performance & Creative Work				
• Read aloud or speak with clarity and expression	•			
• Listen to, and follow, directions	•			
• Use voice and gesture to show a character's feelings	•			
• Interpret the meaning of a play	•	•		
Communication				
• Communicate ideas clearly in writing		•	•	•
• Extend knowledge in creative works (i.e., diary)		•		
• Express point of view in writing, speaking, acting	•	•		•
• Use grade-appropriate writing conventions (i.e., spelling, punctuation, grammar)		•	•	•
• Use well-organized paragraphs		•		
• Write using a variety of forms (i.e., letter, journal, narrative, play)		•		

Table of Contents

Teacher Assessment Rubric

Student's Name: _____

Criteria	Level 1	Level 2	Level 3	Level 4
Understanding Concepts	Demonstrates a limited understanding and interpretation of a play and a character using few related ideas and drama techniques	Demonstrates some understanding and interpretation of a play and a character using some related ideas and some drama techniques	Demonstrates a general understanding and interpretation of a play and a character using clearly related ideas and several drama techniques	Demonstrates a thorough understanding and interpretation of a play and a character with clarity, using relevant ideas, and many appropriate drama techniques
Critical Analysis & Appreciation	Analyses and describes a play/story with limited clarity, using incomplete responses and limited evidence to support ideas	Analyses and describes a play/story with some clarity, using partial responses and some evidence to support ideas	Analyses and describes a play/story with clarity, using complete responses and related evidence to support ideas	Analyses and describes a play/story with detail and clarity, using thorough, well-reasoned responses and relevant evidence to support ideas
	Evaluates and states preferences for plays and performances using incomplete responses and limited evidence to support opinions	Evaluates and states preferences for plays and performances using partial responses and some evidence to support opinions	Evaluates and states preferences for plays and performances using complete responses and appropriate evidence to support opinions	Evaluates and states preferences for plays and performances using thorough, well-reasoned responses and relevant evidence to support opinions
Communication	Communicates ideas and understanding in very limited or incomplete ways	Communicates ideas and understanding with some clarity, but without precision	Usually communicates ideas and understanding with clarity and precision	Communicates ideas and understanding with consistent clarity, precision, and thought
	Communicates using a limited number of writing formats and conventions	Communicates with some accuracy, using a few writing formats and conventions	Communicates with general accuracy, using a variety of writing formats and conventions	Communicates with clarity and accuracy, using a wide variety of writing formats and conventions

Student Self-Assessment Rubric

Name: _____

Put a check mark in the box that best describes your performance. Then, add your points to determine your total score.

	Always 4 Points	Almost Always 3 Points	Sometimes 2 Points	Needs Improvement 1 Point	My Points
✓ I speak and read aloud clearly and with expression.					
✓ I listen well, follow directions, and remain on task during rehearsals, asking for help as needed.					
✓ I express feelings with my voice and gestures.					
✓ I practice my part by reading the script with my group and by reading the script alone during my free time.					
✓ My thoughts and opinions have been expressed clearly, and are supported by ideas from the plays.					
✓ My written work is presented in well-organized paragraphs, and is neat and complete.					
✓ I have revised and edited my work and made corrections.					

Total Points: _____

1. I liked _____

   _____

2. I learned _____

   _____

3. I want to learn more about _____

   _____

Teacher Guide
How to Use This Book

Shakespeare. In most adults, the mention of his name causes a range of reactions, from enthusiasm to confusion as to why we ever bothered to study his works at all. I remember a teacher telling us that learning Shakespeare was "good for us", but I don't ever remember hearing why. Because of this, many have missed out on an appreciation of perhaps the greatest English writer of all time, a writer who understood what it means to be human, a recorder of the vast array of emotions that we all experience – joy, sorrow, love, hate, jealousy, forgiveness, fear, pride, and yet, at the most basic level, a teller of curious, horrifying, sad, and joyous tales that cause us to pause and reflect upon our own experiences and circumstances around us.

Imagine how your appreciation of Shakespeare would have been different if his plays had been introduced to you in simpler forms, much earlier in your school career, letting you experiment with his language, perform as his characters, learn about his historical context, reflect upon the meaning in his plays, and to have, albeit in easy-to-understand terms, an answer to the question "Why do we study Shakespeare?"

This resource attempts to do all of these things through a variety of activities that touch upon the major aspects of a complete Language Arts program: reading, writing, oral language, and drama. **Working with the plays provides students the opportunity to develop confidence with reading, writing, and oral language, as well as drama skills such as performing, rehearsing, mime, and tableau**. These activities support literacy in the most basic sense, in that they allow students to make sense of what they are doing (to understand), and allow them to express themselves in a variety of ways (to be understood). Importantly, the resource introduces children to characters and plotlines that they will encounter time and again, in both higher-grade English classes and in other authors' work. A firm grounding in these enduring themes will allow students to relate one work to another, to find patterns and commonalities, and to construct meaning more effectively.

The eight adapted plays in this resource reflect Shakespeare's plays in their entirety, and have been written using both modern and Shakespearean dialogue, and use narrators to tell the bulk of each story. Some changes, such as reorganizing a scene here and there, toning down violence, or rearranging some lines, have been made to enhance the students' grasp of the story lines. Of note is the fact that the setting of many of these plays is in the distant past, in the ancient civilizations of Rome and Greece, and in both medieval and Renaissance Europe, time periods familiar to the students in these grades through their Social Studies classes.

Three of the plays in this book have also appeared in *Shakespeare Shorts, Grades 2 – 4*, but are presented here in more mature adaptations. *Macbeth, Romeo and Juliet,* and *A Midsummer Night's Dream* have proven to be the most popular adaptations among students at this age level, and adapted as they are for this book, are presented in greater depth, both in character and in plot. Characters who had few or no lines in the younger versions, have complete scenes here. For example, the actors preparing to perform a play for the duke in *A Midsummer Night's Dream* have more dialogue and a new scene from the original play to perform. So, too, do the witches in *Macbeth*, with more lines directly from Shakespeare's original play.

The level of difficulty of the character roles in each play has been indicated as Non-Speaking (NS), Easy (E), Moderate (M), and Challenging (C), to provide teachers with a guideline that will assist in the distribution of roles. Each play is preceded by an introduction with hints on pronunciation, staging, costumes, and possible extension activities that allow children to express their opinions and feelings through a variety of writing activities. A generic comprehension activity is included (page 77) to check each child's grasp of the material they are reading, and a Shakespeare Writing Project (page 78) allows students to take the knowledge and experiences they have acquired and apply them in creative ways.

Each of the plays can be performed with minimal props, costumes, and backgrounds. Most run between 10 and 25 minutes in length, and are very easy to stage. Ideas for a holding a Shakespeare Festival are also included (page 9) which promote the involvement of all members of the class, even those who are very nervous about appearing on stage, because in preparing for a Shakespeare Festival, invitations, programs, and tickets have to be made, as well as decorations, stage setting, props, music, and sound effects.

These plays are meant to be enjoyed by all. I hope that this resource introduces you and your students to them in an exciting way, and allows them to sow the seeds of a life-long appreciation of the works of William Shakespeare.

Two Adapted Scripts for December Holiday Concerts

Two of the plays in this resource are suited to be used as seasonal adaptations, to help with the "What can my class do in our December Holiday concert?" dilemma. *The Comedy of Errors* and *A Midsummer Night's Dream* have been chosen because they are lighter in tone than the tragedies and histories, and because they reflect the spirit common to many religious and secular traditions celebrated at that time of the year: family, reunion, forgiveness, joy, celebration, and peace. *The Comedy of Errors* concerns the separation and reunion of the members of a family from Syracuse, while *A Midsummer Night's Dream* is a playful tale of tricks and love, ending in forgiveness. Both end on a joyous and celebratory note.

Both can be performed on a stage decorated to reflect your school's focus at that time of year, with small lights used to decorate the scene, again reflecting one of the season's more common traditions – a celebration of light.

How to Make the Mini-Book Scripts

The adapted scripts in this resource have been designed to be made quickly and easily into 5½"x 8½" folded booklets, in five steps:

1. Remove the mini-book script from this book.

2. Photocopy the single-sided page of the mini-book that the title of the play (i.e., "Macbeth") appears on ("Page One"). Take the single-sided duplicate page that you have just made, and place it in the paper tray. Now, copy the single-sided page of the mini-book on which "Page Two" appears. You should have a two-sided page with "Page One" on one side, and "Page Two" on the other side. Repeat this step for the remaining pages of the mini-book. You may need to experiment with this step to achieve the proper alignment.

3. Place your duplicated mini-book pages in the same order that they appear in this resource (follow the page numbers in the footer next to "© S&S Learning Materials").

4. Fold in half along the dotted line and staple along the center fold.

5. Model for your students how to assemble the mini-book.

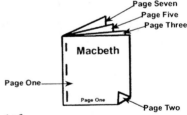

Suggestions for Performing the Plays

As in Shakespeare's day, the best way to prepare for your festival is to keep things simple. Costumes can be put together from things the students already have at home, props should be kept to a minimum (i.e., all weapons are mimed), and the sets/stage decoration can be completed effectively and simply.

Costumes:
Boys' costumes:
Their dad's or their own dress shirt, not tucked in, with belt around the waist; dark pants.

Girls' costumes:
Any kind of longer dress or skirt; if playing a male role, follow the boys' suggestions.

Special costume suggestions:

Nick Bottom's donkey head – please see the special instructions below
Fairies – browns and greens, perhaps with wands and wings
Kings/queens – simply-made crowns, a robe, and a staff; warrior kings could wear a vest to set them apart
Ghosts – white or gray clothing
Witches – witch's hat, dark clothing, pointy nose, etc.
The apparition (*Macbeth*) – ghostly white or gray clothing, or red and black to suggest having risen from the fire and the cauldron

The Comedy of Errors:

To keep the idea that the Ephesus twins are identical, yet have grown up in different towns, try this: have Ephesus of Syracuse wear, for example, a red hat and a blue shirt, and have his brother wear a blue hat and a red shirt. The colors chosen really don't matter, just the fact that they are similar enough that they look alike, and yet are different enough for the audience to tell them apart. For the Dromio twins, choose two other colors (i.e., green and orange) and follow the same pattern as the Ephesus twins.

Props:

Keep the props to a minimum: a letter here and there to be read aloud, and the branches of Birnham Wood and a cauldron for *Macbeth*. These are effective because there aren't too many others to distract from them. Props that are part of a costume (see above) are especially effective. A good rule of thumb: mime props where possible (i.e., swords, knives, etc.).

Sets and Stage Decoration:

Sets can range from none at all, to as detailed as you wish. I have always been fortunate enough to have access to large (approximately 84" x 84") cardboard sheets, donated by a local corrugated paper company. On these sheets, we glue 12" x 18" pieces of construction paper to represent large stones, and decorate them with paper flowers. Some chairs and a decorated bench (or as I have used: stacked gym mats, covered with an old floral shower curtain) usually provide enough decoration. In Shakespeare's day, the stage was enough: the mind, through the words of the characters, created the settings.

How to Make Nick Bottom's Donkey Head
(A Midsummer Night's Dream)

Required Materials
- 11"x 18" construction paper (3 sheets each of brown or gray, black, and yellow)
- 8.5" x 11" blank white paper (2 sheets)
- glue
- stapler
- baseball cap

Steps

1. Curl lengthwise, without a crease, one sheet of brown or gray construction paper, and attach it to a baseball hat with staples. Staple from the inside out, so staples do not scratch the student playing Nick Bottom. This forms the head of the donkey.

2. To make the donkey ears, cut out two long tear drop-shaped ears from the brown or gray paper. Cut out two similarly shaped, but smaller pieces, from the yellow construction paper to make details for the ears. Glue together, and attach to the rear of the donkey's head.

3. To make the donkey's mouth (upper lip only), cut out a piece of yellow in a shape similar to the one shown in the illustration. Add two, white bucked teeth, and nostrils cut from the black construction paper. Attach to the front of the head.

4. To make the donkey's eyes, repeat each of the following steps twice:

    a) Cut out a notched semi-circle using black construction paper for the pupil;

    b) Cut out a rounded white shape as shown, larger than the shape in part a);

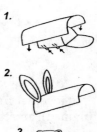

1.

2.

3.

4. a)

4. b)

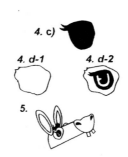

c) Cut out a black shape as shown at right. This is for the eyelid and eyelashes. Make sure it is slightly larger than the white shape in part b);

d) Cut out a slightly jagged, yellow circle, larger than the other shapes; glue them together in order, with a) being the top, and d) being the bottom.

e) Attach to either side of the donkey's head.

5. Add a bushy mane of black construction paper, and enjoy the mask.

Preparing for a Shakespeare Festival

A Shakespeare Festival, the special time when all your efforts are put on display, is really quite easy to prepare. There are two basic components: 1) the plays, and 2) an after-the-plays "feast": a get-together time after the plays have been performed, where snacks are shared, and everyone gets to discuss what they have just seen. It's a nice way to wind down after the excitement of the plays.

Because each play in this resource has so many characters, you may wish to share the plays among an entire grade or division, with one play per class, or as I have done, have students from different classes take on a few roles in a variety of plays.

The time needed to perform all the plays in this book at one time is approximately 1 hour and 45 minutes to 2 hours and 20 minutes. You may choose to perform only four or five of them to meet time constraints.

Here are some of the things to do to prepare for your Shakespeare Festival:

1. **Choose a Date and a Time:** Is the afternoon best, or early in the evening? You may wish, as I have done in the past, to poll the parents for their preferred time.

2. **Letter to Parents:** Create a letter and return form to send to parents to inform them about the upcoming festival. Also ask for their support in the form of donated treats for the after-the-plays "feast".

3. **Invitations:** I have used invitations in the past on a few occasions. They are generally made by folding an 8.5" x 11" piece of paper in half, with the words "You Are Invited..." on the outside, and with a special message from each individual student addressed to his or her parent(s). Individual students decorate their own invitations.

4. **Programs:** The programs I have used have featured the following:
   - a title page
   - a list of the order of performances
   - one page for each play showing the cast, and illustrations made by the students
   - some examples of student writing (i.e., Shakespeare biography, a letter to Shakespeare, etc.)
   - a "The Critics Write" section – a single-page collection of opinions and feelings about the plays written by the classes who attended our dress rehearsals
   - a credits page, thanking all those involved (i.e., the company donating the cardboard for backgrounds, other staff, etc.)

A Brief Shakespeare Biography for Teachers

William Shakespeare lived in a tempestuous time in England's history. When he was born, in 1564, Queen Elizabeth I was on the throne, and England was locked in a firm debate over religion, specifically Roman Catholic versus Protestant, with the result often being violence and execution. The expansion of England's influence around the world had also begun, as explorers such as Sir Francis Drake sailed to far away lands. And as England looked outward, other powers, notably Spain, attempted to check this growing expansion with plans for invasion. At the time of Shakespeare's death, in 1616, James I was on the throne, and his rule was proving unpopular with many groups in English society.

Throughout this period, Shakespeare wrote both plays and poetry that are remembered above the events of the day. And yet, even with this remarkable body of work, we know very little about Shakespeare himself.

Born in Stratford-Upon-Avon, in 1564, the son of a glove maker, John Shakespeare, and his wife, Mary Arden, little remains other than the house in which he was born to tell us of his early years. Educated at the local grammar school, Shakespeare later married Anne Hathaway, a much older woman. They had three children, Susanna, Judith, and Hamnet. Hamnet, his only son, died at the age of eleven. Their marriage appears not to have been a happy one, which might explain why William left for London to find work, and his family remained behind.

In London, Shakespeare acted in several plays, and eventually began writing plays of his own. His plays were rarely original in their conception, often borrowing heavily from other texts. However, in their final form, their use of language, poetry, and a keen insight into human nature, elevated them beyond the other works of his day. Some have even suggested that Shakespeare, with his meager education, was incapable of writing such timeless and thought-provoking works.

Shakespeare wrote four basic kinds of plays: tragedies, comedies, histories, and, what have been called by various names, romances or problem plays. Shakespeare's tragedies are plays in which the hero, or main character, comes to a tragic end because of a flaw in his or her personality, or because of other forces acting on the character which cause the tragedy. Comedies are plays involving humorous situations, mistaken identities, and hilarious turns on figures of speech. They usually end well for all involved, often in a wedding. The history plays are based on great figures from history, and, artistic license aside, are reasonably accurate portrayals of their period. Some, however, portrayed certain historical figures in a negative light, to reflect the prevailing politics of Shakespeare's day. The problem plays, or romances, are often adventurous stories involving difficult problems with interesting resolutions.

Shakespeare is remembered today for the breadth and scope of his work, and also for the subtleties of character and human nature that pervade each play or poem. His influence upon later authors, and the arts in general, is profound, and the rich language and turns of phrase that he coined are used even to this day.

All About William Shakespeare

William Shakespeare was born on April 23, 1564, in the town of Stratford-Upon-Avon, in England. We remember him today, more than 440 years after he was born, for the poems and plays that he wrote.

Very little is known about Shakespeare's childhood, other than that his parents were John Shakespeare and Mary Arden, and that he was educated at the local grammar school. The house in which he was born still stands today. When he was older, Shakespeare married Anne Hathaway, a much older woman, and they had three children, Susanna, Judith, and Hamnet. Unfortunately, Hamnet died when he was only eleven years old.

One day, Shakespeare moved to London, England, and began to write plays. His family remained in Stratford-Upon-Avon. In London, Shakespeare acted in several plays, and eventually began writing plays of his own. He wrote four basic kinds of plays: tragedies, comedies, histories, and, what have been called by various names, romances or problem plays.

Shakespeare's tragedies are plays in which the hero, or main character, comes to a tragic end because of something he or she does, or because of the events around them. *Macbeth*, *Julius Caesar*, and *Romeo and Juliet* are three of his famous tragedies. Shakespeare's comedies are plays involving humorous situations and mistaken identities, which usually end well for all involved, sometimes in a wedding. *The Comedy of Errors* and *A Midsummer Night's Dream* are both famous comedies. The history plays are based on great figures from history, such as kings and knights. *Richard II*, *Henry IV, Part I*, and *Richard III* are all famous plays about English kings from the past. The problem plays, or romances, are often adventurous stories involving difficult problems.

In Shakespeare's time, actors wore interesting costumes, a few wore masks, and they used some props, like guns or swords. If you were an actor working with Shakespeare, you might have to be a king, a soldier, a witch, a fairy, or a ghost. Only men and boys could be in the plays, because people in Shakespeare's day thought it was rude for a woman or a girl to be in a play. Since girls were not allowed, boys got to play the parts of the ladies!

One of the theaters Shakespeare worked in was called The Globe. It could hold 3 000 people, and was a theater without a roof! Rich people sat on benches in a covered area, but most people stood on the floor and watched the plays. The people who stood were called groundlings, and if it rained, they got wet! When they didn't like a play, they often threw things at the actors.

Shakespeare returned to Stratford-Upon-Avon when he was much older, after a fire burned The Globe Theatre to the ground. He died when he was 52, on his birthday, April 23, in 1616. When he died, many people mourned him.

We remember him today because he wrote plays that continue to mean a lot to us. Plays like *Richard III*, *Romeo and Juliet*, and *A Midsummer Night's Dream* are still performed everywhere, because people like to hear the ideas and words that Shakespeare wrote, and because he told stories about the feelings that people have always had.

A Guide to Shakespearean Vocabulary

Shakespeare is often difficult for people today to understand because of the language used in his day. Below you will find examples of some of the common "old-fashioned" words and phrases used by Shakespeare, with modern explanations. Once you understand them, Shakespeare's plays will be even more enjoyable to you.

Word	Meaning	Example	Meaning
thou	you	**Thou** shalt be king.	**You** shall be king.
thee	you	I give this to **thee**.	I give this to **you**.
thy	your	I see **thy** glory.	I see **your** glory.
hast	have	…try all thy friends thou **hast** in Ephesus.	…try all your friends you **have** in Ephesus.
hath	has	His majesty **hath** appointed this …	His majesty **has** appointed this…
art	are	O, Bottom, thou **art** changed!	Oh, Bottom, you **are** changed!
wilt	will	**Wilt** thou be gone?	**Will** you go?
dost	do	What **dost** thou know?	What **do** you know?
shalt	shall	Thou **shalt** be king.	You **shall** be king.
'tis	it is	**'Tis** he, that villain Romeo.	**It is** he, that villain Romeo.
whence	where	**Whence** is that knocking?	**Where** is that knocking coming from?
hence	from here	Help me **hence**!	Help me **from here**!
whither	where	**Whither** have they vanished?	**Where** have they vanished to?

Shakespeare also uses some old-fashioned verb forms not listed above. Since Shakespeare often wrote in a form of verse that had to have a certain number of beats in each line to maintain its rhythm, he often used what we would call contractions to make the words fit. For example, you might see the words **speakest** (pronounced *speak-ist*), which means "speak", and **speak'st** (pronounced as *speakst*) in a different place. They both mean the same thing. Another example is the use of past tense verbs ending in -ed. In order to fit into the beats per line of his verse, Shakespeare often replaces the "e" with an apostrophe. You might see the words **punished** and **punish'd** in the same play, and while they have the same meaning, they are pronounced very differently. **Punished** is pronounced *pun-ish-ed*, a three-syllable word, while **punish'd** is pronounced the same way as we would pronounce the word *punished*. In this collection of plays, do not pronounce the –ed ending as a separate syllable unless specifically told to do so.

Richard II

Performance Length	*Number of Parts*	*Genre*
10 to 15 Minutes	15	History

Synopsis

Long ago, in England, the young king, Richard II was proving to be unpopular for his arrogant decisions and pursuits. The final straw for many of the nobles occurred when Richard seized the inheritance of Henry Bolingbroke, his cousin who he had earlier banished, to finance an armed assault on some rebel Irish. Upon returning to England, Richard found his reign opposed almost universally, and several of his supporters already executed. Surrendering his crown to Bolingbroke, Richard was sent to the Tower of London, where he was assassinated by a supporter of Bolingbroke, now King Henry IV. Saddened by the news of Richard's death, Henry promised to go on a pilgrimage to the Holy Land to atone for his role in Richard's demise.

Characters

Reading Levels of Difficulty:
Non-Speaking (NS)   **Easy (E)**   **Moderate (M)**   **Challenging (C)**

King Richard II **(C)**
John of Gaunt **(C)**
Aumerle **(M)**
Bushy **(E)**
Duke of York **(C)**
Sir Stephen Scroop **(E)**
Northumberland **(E)**
Narrator **(M)**

Henry Bolingbroke, Duke of Hereford **(C)**
Thomas Mowbray, Duke of Norfolk **(C)**
Green **(E)**
Bagot **(NS)**
Earl of Salisbury **(E)**
Henry Percy, or Hotspur **(NS)**
Sir Pierce of Exton **(M)**

Pronunciation Guide

Aumerle (ah-murl or oh-murl)

Staging & Costumes

The staging can be accomplished very simply. Props are very simple: a crown, and a throne for the king. Weapons are mimed. Northumberland must read from a scrolled sheet of paper. At the beginning of the play, have King Richard wear bright colors, such as red or royal blue, but after he gives up his throne, to emphasize his reduced position and sadness, have him change into a darker colored costume prior to him greeting Bolingbroke at Flint castle. King Richard should also be portrayed as a more sympathetic character after he abdicates, and those around Bolingbroke as very eager to have achieved power. Have the student playing Richard try to appear calm yet regal in the face of his changed position, and the student playing Bolingbroke to appear ashamed by his supporters' actions.

Teaching Tips

• Discuss what is meant by a history play.
• Discuss briefly the constant struggle for the throne of England during the Middle Ages.
• Brainstorm ideas about "What is a hero?". Who is the hero in this play? Is there one?

Extension Activities

• Retell the story as a newspaper article or as a TV news report, highlighting the major events.
• Draw a picture of your favorite scene in the play/write a paragraph telling why you chose it.
• Complete a survey: Do you feel sorry for King Richard? Ask for reasons. Present your information and findings to the class.

Richard II

Dramatis Personae

King Richard II –

Henry Bolingbroke,

Duke of Hereford –

John of Gaunt –

Thomas Mowbray,

Duke of Norfolk –

Aumerle –

Green –

Bushy –

Bagot –

Duke of York –

Earl of Salisbury –

Sir Stephen Scroop –

Henry Percy, or Hotspur –

Northumberland –

Sir Pierce of Exton –

Narrator –

King Richard: How now? What means death in this rude assault? Villain, thine own hand yields thy death's instrument. *(King Richard takes one of the men's knives and stabs him. The man falls, but as King Richard watches, Exton stabs him. King Richard points to Exton's knife.)* That hand shall burn in never-quenching fire. Mount, mount my soul, while my flesh sinks down, here to die. *(He dies.)*

Later, as Bolingbroke, now King Henry sat in his throne room, Exton came in bearing the dead body of King Richard.

Bolingbroke: What is this?

Sir Pierce of Exton: Great king, within this coffin I present thy buried fear: Richard of Bordeaux, thy greatest enemy.

Bolingbroke: Exton, I thank thee not. This is a deed of slander on my head. My guilt is great, because I wished him dead. Lords, I protest my soul is full of woe. I'll make a voyage to the Holy Land, to wash this blood off from my guilty hand. March sadly after, grace my mournings here, in weeping after this untimely bier.

Long ago, in England, the young king, Richard II, often ruled in an arrogant way. Unlike his father, King Edward, Richard did not always take the advice of wiser men around him, and so he often made decisions that would come back to haunt him.

King Richard: Old John of Gaunt, call them to our presence, Bolingbroke and Norfolk, and face to face, frowning brow to frowning brow, we will hear them.

John of Gaunt: Bring them in.

(Enter Bolingbroke and Norfolk.)

Bolingbroke: *(Bows.)* Many happy days befall my gracious sovereign.

Norfolk: *(Bows.)* Each day still better other's happiness.

King Richard: We thank you both. Cousin Bolingbroke, what dost thou object against the Duke of Norfolk, Thomas Mowbray?

Bolingbroke: Free from misbegotten hate, come I before your princely presence. Thomas Mowbray is a traitor. He took your money and did wrongly use it, and plotted the Duke of Gloucester's death.

Bolingbroke: Are you contented to resign the crown?

King Richard: Ay, no. No, ay. I give this heavy weight from off my head, and this unwieldy scepter from my hand. God save King Henry, unkinged Richard says. What more remains?

Northumberland: No more, but read over these accusations, and these grievous crimes committed by your person.

King Richard: Must I do so? Mine eyes are full of tears.

Northumberland: My lord, read over these articles.

King Richard: Fiend! Thou tormentest me ere I come.

Bolingbroke: Enough, Northumberland. Convey him to the Tower. *(Exit Richard and Northumberland.)* On Wednesday next, we solemnly set down our coronation.

As he was taken to prison in the Tower, Richard sent his wife to France to save her life, but she was very unhappy to leave him. Unknown to Bolingbroke, now King Henry IV, a man named Sir Pierce of Exton, a loyal servant of his, had decided to kill King Richard in his Tower prison cell, because he had once heard Bolingbroke say that he wished King Richard dead. As King Richard sat in his cell, Exton and two men entered with knives drawn.

King Richard: How high a pitch his resolution soars! Thomas Mowbray, what say'st thou to this?

Norfolk: Bolingbroke, thou liest! I defy you, and spit at you, and call you a slanderous coward and a villain. The money I used to go to France to fetch the queen, and as for Gloucester's death, I slew him not.

King Richard: Good uncle, let's end this where it begun, we'll calm the Duke of Norfolk, you, your son.

John of Gaunt: To be a peacemaker shall become my age. My son, end this argument.

King Richard: Norfolk, you do likewise.

Norfolk: My name is disgraced here, pierced to the soul. I cannot.

King Richard: Cousin Bolingbroke, do you begin?

Bolingbroke: I cannot.

King Richard: We were not born to sue, but to command. Our kingdom's earth shall not be soiled with blood. Therefore, we banish you both from our territories. You, cousin Bolingbroke, upon pain of death, twice five summers must you stay away.

Page Three

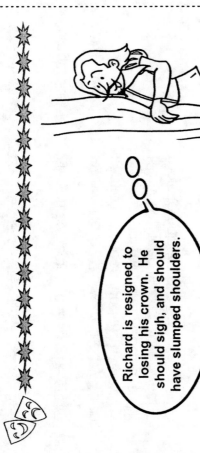

Richard is resigned to losing his crown. He should sigh, and should have slumped shoulders.

As they neared Flint Castle, Bolingbroke and his supporters were surprised to find that the king was inside. After a brief wait, King Richard came down to see Bolingbroke, knowing he was going to lose his kingdom to him.

King Richard: Your heart is up, although your knee be low.

Bolingbroke: My gracious lord, I come but for my own.

King Richard: Your own is yours, and I am yours, and all. What thou will have, I'll give, and willing too. Are we going to London?

Bolingbroke: Yea, my good lord.

King Richard: Then I must not say no.

In London, King Richard willingly surrendered his crown to Bolingbroke.

Page Ten

Bolingbroke: Your will be done. This must my comfort be, that sun, that warms you here, shall shine on me.

King Richard: Norfolk, for thee remains a heavier doom. The hopeless word of – Never to return, breathe I against thee, upon pain of death.

Norfolk: A heavy sentence, my most sovereign liege. And unlooked for from your highness' mouth. Then must I turn me from my country's light, to dwell in solemn shades of endless night.

King Richard: Swear, both, to keep the oath we administer: never to look upon each other's face, and never to plot, or contrive any ill against us, our state, our subjects, or our land.

Bolingbroke: I swear.

Norfolk: And I, to keep all this.

Bolingbroke: I swear.

After each man had left the kingdom, King Richard called his closest advisors, Bushy, Bagot, and Green to his side. His cousin Aumerle was also there.

Green: My lord, now we must deal with the rebels in Ireland.

Page Four

Aumerle: While you were away, Bolingbroke has returned, and grows strong and great, in substance and in power.

(Enter Earl of Salisbury. Bows.)

King Richard: Welcome, my lord Salisbury. How far off is your power?

Earl of Salisbury: Today overthrows thy joys, friends, fortunes, and thy state. The Welshmen, thinking thou wert dead, are gone to Bolingbroke, dispersed, and fled.

(Enter Sir Stephen Scroop. Bows.)

King Richard: What has become of Bushy? Where is Green?

Aumerle: They are dead?

Sir Stephen Scroop: They lie full low, graved in hollow ground.

Aumerle: They are dead?

Sir Stephen Scroop: Yea, all of them lost their heads.

King Richard: I cannot fight this. Let us sit upon the ground and tell sad stories of the death of kings. I will go to Flint Castle, and there I'll pine away, and that power I have, discharge.

Page Nine

King Richard: We will ourself in person to this war, but our coffers are grown somewhat light. We are enforced to farm our royal realm; the revenue whereof shall furnish us for affairs in hand.

(Enter Bushy.)

Bushy: *(Bows.)* Old John of Gaunt is grievous sick, and entreats your majesty to visit him at Ely-house.

King Richard: If he dies, we can use his coffers to fight these Irish wars. Come gentlemen, let's all go visit him.

At John of Gaunt's house, the old man grew gravely ill. With him was King Richard's other uncle, the Duke of York.

John of Gaunt: Will the king come, that I may breathe my last in wholesome council to his unstaid youth?

Duke of York: All in vain comes council to his ear.

John of Gaunt: Methinks I am a prophet new inspired to tell him that his rash decisions will consume him and this royal throne of kings, this sceptered isle, this blessed plot, this earth, this realm, this England.

Page Five

Bolingbroke: I was banished as Bolingbroke, Duke of Hereford, but as I come, I come for Lancaster.

Duke of York: You cherish rebellion, and are rebels all. However, I do remain as neuter, for I am loth to break our country's laws, and will remain in my castle.

Hearing of the approach of Bolingbroke while waiting for King Richard to return, the Earl of Salisbury feared for his king. To make matters worse, two of King Richard's loyal men, Bushy and Green, were captured by Bolingbroke, and sentenced to death as traitors for misleading King Richard.

Bolingbroke: See them delivered to execution and the hand of death.

Bushy: More welcome is the stroke of death to me than Bolingbroke to England.

Green: My comfort is, that Heaven will take our souls.

Returning to the coast of Wales, King Richard met with his cousin Aumerle.

Page Eight

Page Six

(Enter King Richard, Aumerle, Bushy, Bagot, and Green.)

King Richard: How is it with aged Gaunt?

John of Gaunt: Old Gaunt, indeed. Gaunt I am for the grave. But take this counsel: A thousand flatterers sit within thy crown, Landlord of England art thou now, not king. You are my brother Edward's son, but live in thy shame. These words hereafter thy tormentors be. Convey me to my bed, then to my grave.

(Exit John of Gaunt, aided by attendants.)

Duke of York: I do beseech your majesty, impute his words to sickliness and age in him. He loves you, on my life, and holds you dear.

King Richard: Right, you say true.

(Enter Duke of Northumberland.)

Duke of Northumberland: My lord, John of Gaunt is dead. Words, life, and all, old Lancaster hath spent.

Duke of York: Though death be poor, it ends a mortal woe.

Page Seven

King Richard: Now that he is dead, towards our assistance do we seize to us all that old Gaunt possessed.

Richard's decision here leads to his downfall. The Duke of York's words are very important.

Duke of York: Do not take what now belongs to Bolingbroke, his son and heir. You may lose a thousand well-disposed hearts by doing so.

King Richard: Think what you will, we seize into our hands his plate, his goods, his money, his lands.

Duke of York: I'll not be by the while. My liege, farewell. What will ensue hereof, none can tell.

While King Richard journeyed to Ireland, many of the nobles and lords grew angry with his decision to take Bolingbroke's inheritance. When news came to them that Bolingbroke was returning to England with an army to claim his inheritance and title, the Duke of Lancaster, they rode off to join him. Northumberland, his son Harry Percy, also known as Hotspur, and others were welcomed into Bolingbroke's camp. Even King Richard's uncle, the Duke of York, deserted his post.

Henry IV, Part 1

Performance Length	Number of Parts	Genre
10 to 15 Minutes	14	History

Synopsis

Following the death of Richard II, King Henry IV decides to make a pilgrimage to the Holy Land to atone for his part in Richard's death. However, after finding out that there are uprisings against his throne, and that several of the nobles who helped him become king are becoming mutinous, he cancels his journey to deal with these problems at home. Meanwhile, his son, Prince Henry, is living a life that embarrasses his father, by hanging around with cutpurses, such as Sir John Falstaff, in pubs around London. Eventually, Prince Henry casts aside these poor behaviors and joins his father to defeat the rebels that threaten his crown. The play ends with the major threats disbanded or killed, and the king welcoming the changes in his son.

Characters

Reading Levels of Difficulty:
Non-Speaking (NS)   Easy (E)   Moderate (M)   Challenging (C)

King Henry IV **(C)**

Prince Henry (Hal), his son **(C)**

Sir John Falstaff **(C)**

Gadshill **(E)**

Peto **(E)**

Earl of Westmoreland **(M)**

Prince John **(E)**

Earl of Northumberland **(M)**

Henry Percy (Hotspur), his son **(C)**

Poins **(C)**

Bardolph **(E)**

Earl of Worcester **(M)**

Sir Henry Blunt **(E)**

Narrator **(M)**

Pronunciation Guide

Worcester (wus-ter)

Staging & Costumes

The staging can be accomplished very simply. Props are very simple: a crown, a small cloth bag full of pretend money, and, perhaps, a throne for the king. Weapons are mimed. Costumes are similar to other play suggestions (see page 7 of the Teacher Guide).

Teaching Tips

• Discuss what is meant by a history play. What are the characteristics of a history play? How is it different from a tragedy or a comedy? Compare the three in a chart form.

• Discuss briefly the constant struggle for the throne of England during the Middle Ages.

• Brainstorm ideas about "What is a hero?". Who is the hero in this play? Is there one?

Extension Activities

• Retell the story as a newspaper article or as a TV news report, highlighting the brave deeds.

• Draw a picture of your favorite scene in the play/write a paragraph telling why you chose it.

• What is your opinion? When Prince Henry decides to change his poor behavior, does he betray his friend Falstaff, or does he simply take on the responsibilities of someone who will eventually become king? Or is it a combination of both?

Henry IV, Part I

Dramatis Personae

King Henry IV – _____

Prince Henry (Hal), his son – _____

Earl of Northumberland – _____

Henry Percy (Hotspur), his son – _____

Sir John Falstaff – _____

Poins – _____

Gadshill – _____

Bardolph – _____

Peto – _____

Earl of Worcester – _____

Earl of Westmoreland – _____

Sir Henry Blunt – _____

Prince John – _____

Narrator – _____

Page One

Prince John: But soft, whom have we here? Did you not tell me this fat man was dead?

Prince Henry: Art thou alive? I saw you dead!

Falstaff: No, I have killed Hotspur, and have come for my reward.

Prince Henry: Why, Percy I killed myself, and saw thee dead!

Prince John: This is the strangest tale that ever I heard.

Prince Henry: This is the strangest fellow, brother. *(Laughing.)* Come, Jack, let's see what can be done.

Later in the King's camp, King Henry was pleased with the change in his son. To bring peace to the land, plans were made to chase down the rebels in Wales and to the north.

King Henry: There is still much to do so that rebellion in this land shall lose his way. You, son John, and my cousin Westmoreland, towards York shall bend you, and myself and Prince Henry, will towards Wales. Let us not leave till all our own be won.

Page Twelve

Following the abdication and murder of King Richard II, the new king, King Henry IV, began his rule in England with a promise to make a journey to the Holy Land to atone for his part in Richard's death. However, he soon had to change his plans and cancel his pilgrimage, as some of the nobles who helped him take the crown began to turn against him.

King Henry is truly sorry for Richard's death, and not being able to go on his pilgrimage bothers him a lot.

King Henry: It seems then that the tidings of this broil break off our business for the Holy Land.

Westmoreland: Even more unwelcome news comes from the north. Gallant Hotspur, young Harry Percy, has defeated the Scots, and taken prisoners, but he has refused to give them over to you, my liege.

King Henry: He is a fine young man, while only riot and dishonor stain the brow of my young Harry. Nevertheless, what think you of this young Percy's pride? Why does he keep the prisoners?

Westmoreland: This is his uncle's teachings, this is Worcester, malevolent to you in all aspects.

Page Two

Prince Henry: Thou speakest as if I would deny my name.

Hotspur: My name is Harry Percy.

Prince Henry: Then we shall fight!

(They fight with swords and Prince Henry kills Hotspur.)

Hotspur: O, Harry, thou hast robbed me of my youth and life. The cold hand of death lies on my tongue. *(He dies.)*

Prince Henry: Fare thee well, great heart! *(He turns and sees Falstaff lying on the ground.)* What, old acquaintance! Poor Jack, farewell. In blood by noble Percy lie.

As Prince Henry left the battlefield, Falstaff sat up and looked around, and saw Hotspur dead.

Falstaff: The better part of valor is discretion, in which better part, I have saved my life. *(Stands.)* Zounds, I am afraid of this gunpowder Percy, thou he be dead.

Seeing Hotspur dead, Falstaff made up a plan, and pretended to kill Hotspur. He then picked him up, and carried him away on his back. He took the body to Prince Henry and his brother, Prince John, hoping for a reward.

Page Eleven

King Henry: Bring them to me on Wednesday, to Windsor, at our next council.

Westmoreland: I will, my liege.

In another part of London, in a tavern, Henry, Prince of Wales, or as his friends called him, Prince Hal, sat with Sir John Falstaff, a rotund and jolly fellow.

> Falstaff is one of Shakespeare's most popular characters. He should be shown as full of mischief, yet not always as brave as he pretends.

Falstaff: Now, Hal, what time of day is it, lad?

Prince Henry: Thou art so fat-witted, why ask for the time of day?

Falstaff: Because we that take purses, go by the moon. When thou art king, sweet wag, let us not, that are squires of the night, be called thieves – let us be called "gentlemen of the shade" or "minions of the moon".

(Enter Poins.)

Prince Henry: Good morrow, Ned.

Page Three

Prince Henry: (To the audience.) I do, I will.

Later, in King Henry's castle, the king summoned his son before him. Speaking with his father, Prince Henry promised to change his ways and behave more like a prince should.

King Henry: Thou hast lost thy princely privilege with vile participation.

Prince Henry: I am sorry. I shall hereafter, my thrice gracious lord, be more myself.

King Henry: Good, because Hotspur and his traitorous friends are planning to attack us.

Prince Henry: I will redeem all this on Percy's head, and in the closing of some glorious day, be bold to tell you that I am your son.

As Prince Henry left for battle, he called Poins, Falstaff, Bardolph, Peto, and Gadshill to fight with him. He even made Falstaff a captain, and put him in charge of a group of fighting men! However, Falstaff had a habit of falling down and playing dead to avoid fighting in the battle!

On the battlefield, Prince Henry met Hotspur, and they had a terrible sword fight.

Hotspur: If I mistake not, thou art Prince Henry.

Page Ten

Prince Henry: Good morrow, sweet Hal. I have heard that, by four o'clock tomorrow, there are pilgrims going to Canterbury with rich offerings, and traders riding to London with fat purses. If you come, I'll stuff your purses full of crowns. Will you come?

Prince Henry: Who, I rob? I a thief? Not I.

Falstaff: Wonderful! Meet us at Eastcheap tomorrow. Now, Sir John, I prithee leave the prince and me alone, so I may convince him to come.

Poins: I will!

Falstaff: Farewell! You shall find me in Eastcheap. *(Exit Falstaff.)*

Poins: Ride with me, my good lord, for I have a jest to execute. Falstaff, Bardolph, Peto, and Gadshill shall rob these men, and then you and I, in disguise, shall rob them! Our four friends will flee in terror. The virtue of the jest will be the incomprehensible lies that this same fat rogue will tell us. He'll say how 30 attacked them, and how they fought them off. What fun it will be!

Prince Henry: Well, I'll go with thee. I'll meet you in Eastcheap. Farewell.

Poins: Farewell, my lord. *(Exit Poins.)*

Page Four

Prince Henry: What, fought ye with them all? I pray you have not murdered some of them.

Falstaff: Nay.

Prince Henry: Well, breathe a little, and hear me speak but this. We saw you four rob four, and become masters of their wealth. Then did we two set on you four, and have the money here to prove it. *(laughing.)* Falstaff, you carried your guts away nimbly and with dexterity, roaring for mercy!

Falstaff: I knew it was thee as well as he that made thee. Would I kill the heir apparent? *(laughing.)* We shall be merry, now that our money is returned. *(Everyone laughs.)* Hal, take me with you when you become king.

Prince Henry: Banish Peto, banish Bardolph, banish Poins; but for sweet Jack Falstaff, banish not him thy Harry's company. Banish plump Jack and banish all the world.

(Exit all but Prince Henry.)

Prince Hall is very serious here. He knows he will have to turn his back on his friend when he becomes King.

Page Nine

Prince Henry: *(To the audience.)*
One day I'll throw off this loose behavior, and my reformation shall show more goodly, and attract more eyes than that which hath no foil to set it off. It will be a redeeming time, when men think least I will.

In King Henry's castle, The Earl of Northumberland, Hotspur, Worcester, and Sir Henry Blunt, stood before the king to answer for their actions.

King Henry: You tread upon my patience.

Worcester: We little deserve this, we who helped make you king.

King Henry: Worcester, get thee gone, for I do see danger and disobedience in thine eye. When we need your use and counsel, we shall send for them.

(Exit Worcester.)

Northumberland: My son is guilty of nothing.

Hotspur: My liege, I did deny no prisoners. After the battle, when I was dry with rage, came a certain lord, neat and trimly dressed, demanding my prisoners, in your majesty's behalf. Smarting,

Page Five

(Enter Falstaff, Bardolph, Peto, and Gadshill.)

Poins: Welcome, Jack. Where hast thou been?

Falstaff: Where were you? I call thee cowards.

Prince Henry: What's the matter?

> Falstaff's story changes as he tells it. He should tell it with a lot of drama and broad gestures.

Falstaff: We four have taken a thousand pound this night.

Prince Henry: Where is it, Jack?

Falstaff: Taken from us, by a hundred men!

Prince Henry: What, a hundred men?

Falstaff: I swung my sword and cut through and through, thrusting and hacking like a hand saw!

Gadshill: We bound them.

Peto: No, they were not bound.

Falstaff: They were, every man of them.

Page Eight

with my wounds being cold, I answered neglectingly, I know not what.

Sir Henry Blunt: Good my lord, what then he said, so he unsay it now.

King Henry: Send me your prisoners with the speediest means, or you shall hear in such a kind from me as will displease you. My lord, Northumberland, you and your son may leave. Send us your prisoners, or you'll hear of it.

(Exit King Henry and Blunt.)

Hotspur: I will not send them!

(Enter Worcester.)

Northumberland: *(To Worcester.)* Brother, the king hath made your nephew mad.

Worcester: Peace, cousin, say no more. Let us use those same noble Scots that are your prisoners to help us raise an army against the king.

Hotspur: We'll be revenged on him for this, and put the Earl of Mortimer on the throne, as dead King Richard had wished, when he

Page Six

proclaimed him heir to the crown before he died.

Worcester: Cousins, farewell. Say no more of this. By letters I shall direct your course.

Northumberland: Farewell, good brother. We shall thrive, I trust.

Hotspur: Uncle, adieu.

Later that night, Prince Hal and Poins hid near the road to Canterbury, waiting for Falstaff and his fellow thieves to come along after having robbed the travelers on the road. They hear them, walking along and sharing the money.

Poins: Stand close, I hear them coming.

Prince Henry: *(Jumping out.)* Your money!

Poins: *(Jumping out.)* Villains!

Falstaff, Bardolph, Peto, and Gadshill: *(Yelling.)* Ahh! *(They run away.)*

Bardolph, Peto, and Gadshill ran away instantly, and after only a blow or two, Falstaff joined them, leaving their money behind. Later, at a tavern in Eastcheap, Prince Hal and Poins heard Falstaff's account of what had happened to them.

Page Seven

Richard III

Performance Length	Number of Parts	Genre
10 to 15 Minutes	20	History

Synopsis

Long ago, in England, two noble families struggled for control of the English throne. The House of Lancaster, with its emblem of a white rose, and the House of York, its symbol being a red rose, plotted against one another for the crown in a struggle known as The War of the Roses. While King Edward IV sat upon the throne, a struggle for power began within his own family, within the House of York. Richard, Duke of Gloucester, became jealous of his brother's power, and decided to plan and scheme until the crown was his. Doing away with his brother Clarence, thereby aiding in the death of King Edward, and murdering Edward's two sons, Richard is crowned King Richard III. But as soon as the crown is his, the House of Lancaster, under the leadership of Henry, Earl of Richmond, raises an army, defeats Richard, and claims the throne as their own.

Characters

Reading Levels of Difficulty:
Non-Speaking (NS)   Easy (E)   Moderate (M)   Challenging (C)

House of York:
King Edward IV **(E)**
His sons:
Edward, Prince of Wales **(M)**
Richard, Duke of York **(M)**
His brothers:
Richard, Duke of Gloucester,
later King Richard III **(C)**
George, Duke of Clarence **(E)**
Queen Elizabeth **(M)**
Duchess of York **(M)**
Queen Anne **(M)**
Narrator **(M)**

House of Lancaster:
Henry, Earl of Richmond, later King Henry VII **(M)**
Queen Margaret **(E)**
Lord **(E)**
Others:
Lord Grey **(M)**
Lord Stanley **(E)**
Duke of Buckingham **(E)**
Lord Rivers **(M)**
Murderer 1 **(E)**
Murderer 2 **(E)**
Ratcliff **(E)**
James Tyrrel **(E)**

Pronunciation Guide

Gloucester (gloss-ter)

Staging & Costumes

The staging can be accomplished very simply. Props are very simple: a crown and a throne for the king. Weapons are mimed. King Richard should walk with a slightly hunched back or a limp, because Shakespeare portrayed him in this way in the original play to reinforce his evil nature. Costumes are similar to other play suggestions, but Richard's supporters could be identified by a red rose, slightly larger than a poppy, pinned to their costumes. Similarly, Richmond and the Lancasters, could be identified by a white rose, slightly larger than a poppy, pinned to their costumes.

Teaching Tips

- Discuss what is meant by a history play.
- Discuss briefly the constant struggle for the throne of England during the Middle Ages and Renaissance, focusing on the War of the Roses, and looking in the symbols used by each.
- Brainstorm ideas about "What is a villain?". Who is the villain in this play? Compare King Richard to other villains in movies, stories, and on TV.

Extension Activities

- Retell the story as a newspaper article or as a TV news report, highlighting the major events.
- Draw a picture of your favorite scene in the play/write a paragraph telling why you chose it.
- Complete a survey: Does King Richard get what he deserves in the end? Ask for reasons. Present your information and findings to the class.

Richard III

Dramatis Personae

House of York:
King Edward IV – _____

His sons:
Edward, Prince of Wales – _____
Richard, Duke of York – _____

His brothers:
Richard, Duke of Gloucester,
later King Richard III – _____
George, Duke of Clarence – _____
Queen Elizabeth – _____
Duchess of York – _____
Queen Anne – _____

House of Lancaster:
Henry, Earl of Richmond,
later King Henry VII – _____
Queen Margaret – _____
Lord – _____

Others:
Lord Grey – _____
Lord Stanley – _____
Duke of Buckingham – _____
Lord Rivers – _____
Murderer 1 – _____
Murderer 2 – _____
Ratcliff – _____
James Tyrrel – _____
Narrator – _____

Page One

The battle was long and hard-fought. With his horse killed, King Richard spent his time on foot looking for Richmond, but he could not find him. Finally, as his forces faced defeat, and his enemies surrounded him, King Richard realized that his only chance of continuing the battle was to get another horse.

King Richard: A horse! A horse! My kingdom for a horse!

However, his cries were to no avail, and only attracted Richmond to him. In a sword fight, Richmond slew the king, and King Richard fell to the ground, dead.

Richmond: Victorious friends, the day is ours, the bloody dog is dead!

As the fighting ended, Richmond, of the House of Lancaster, and Elizabeth, widow of Edward IV, of the House of York, were married, and the two houses were united in peace.

Page Twelve

Long ago, in England, two noble families struggled for control of the English throne. The House of Lancaster, which included such kings as Henry IV and Henry V, was proud of its emblem: a white rose. And the House of York, among them King Edward IV, held high its symbol: a red rose. And so this struggle became known as The War of the Roses.

While King Edward IV sat upon the throne, a struggle for power began within his own family, within the House of York. Richard, Duke of Gloucester, became jealous of his brother's power, and decided to plan and scheme until the crown was his.

Gloucester: Now is the winter of our discontent made glorious summer by this son of York. I, that am not shaped for sportive tricks, have no delight to pass away the time like my brother, King Edward. And therefore, I am determined to prove a villain. Plots have I laid, lies and deceits, to set my brother Clarence and the king in deadly hate against each other, leading the king to believe that "G" will murder him. But dive down thoughts, here George, Duke of Clarence comes.
(Enter George, Duke of Clarence, guarded.)
Brother, good day. What means this armed guard?

Ghost of Queen Anne: *(To King Richard.)* Despair and die. *(To Richmond.)* Thy adversary's wife doth pray for thee!

(King Richard wakes. Enter Ratcliff.)

King Richard: Who's there?

Ratcliff: My lord, 'tis I. Your friends buckle on their armor.

King Richard: In my dreams methought the souls of all that I murdered came to my tent, and every one did threat vengeance on the head of Richard. O, Ratcliff, I fear, I fear.

(Exit King Richard and Ratcliff. As they leave, Richmond awakes, as a lord enters.)

Lord: Good morrow, Richmond. How have you slept, my lord?

Richmond: The sweetest sleep, and fairest-boding dreams. In my dreams methought the souls of all that Richard had murdered came to my tent, and cried on victory. 'Tis time to arm!

Clarence: His majesty hath appointed this conduct to convey me to the Tower because my name, George, starts with the letter G.

Gloucester: Alack, that is no fault of yours. But what's the matter? May I know?

Clarence: This king thinks that someone whose name starts with G will murder him.

Gloucester: Well, your imprisonment will not be long. I will deliver you.
(Exit Clarence and guards.)
My plan is working! Go, Clarence, and never return, for I will shortly send thy soul to Heaven!

Later that day, as the body of the former king, Henry VI, was carried away to be buried, Richard caught sight of Anne, the old king's widow. She hated Richard, because he had killed her husband. However, with charming words, Richard convinced her that he was not evil, and would make a good husband for her.

Richard deceives Anne with false kindness. He should speak to her in a sweet manner, but change to an angry voice once she leaves.

Page Three

On the night before the battle, as King Richard slept, the ghosts of all of those he had killed appeared before him and wished him ill. They also appeared before Henry, Earl of Richmond, and wished him well.

[Have Richard sleeping on one side of the stage, and Henry on the other. The ghosts should enter at the center and speak to each man in turn, and then leave the stage.]

Richard should toss and turn in silence as each ghost speaks to him.

Ghost of Henry VI: *(To King Richard.)* King Henry bids you despair and die.
(To Richmond.) Richmond, sleep, live, and flourish!

Ghosts of Rivers and Grey: *(To King Richard.)* Despair and die.
(To Richmond.) Richmond, awake and win the day!

Ghosts of the two young princes: *(To King Richard.)* Thy nephews' souls bid thee despair and die.
(To Richmond.) Richmond, sleep, and wake in joy! Edward's unhappy sons bid thee flourish!

Page Ten

Anne: What black magician conjures up this fiend? Lady Margaret saw you kill my husband!

Gloucester: Here, take my sword, and here is my chest. It was I that killed him, and humbly beg death upon my knee for it.
(Anne raises the sword to strike.)
But it was thy beauty, thy heavenly face, that set me on.
(Anne slowly lowers the sword.)

Anne: Arise. Though I wish your death, I will not be thy executioner. I would I knew thy heart.

Gloucester: This will show you. Please wear this ring.
(Hands her a ring.) I am sorry for what I have done.

Anne: It much joys me to see you are become so penitent. Farewell.

(Exit Anne.)

Gloucester: I will have her as my wife, but I will not keep her long! I that killed her husband!

In the castle, King Edward was not well, and his wife, Queen Elizabeth, grew concerned. Several loyal men, Rivers, Grey, Buckingham, and Stanley, tried their best to console her.

Page Four

Gloucester: Why, what should you fear?

York: My uncle Clarence's angry ghost!

Prince: I fear no uncles dead.

With the princes in the Tower, Richard began spreading rumors that they were not really the children of dead King Edward, and were really a threat to the English throne. When the people heard this, many believed it, and Richard was crowned King Richard III. One of his first acts as king was to have the princes murdered. For this evil task, he hired James Tyrrel.

King Richard: Do you resolve to kill a friend of mine?

Tyrrel: I had rather kill two enemies.

King Richard: Then do away with those princes in the Tower.

When it was discovered that the princes were dead, the Duchess of York and Queen Elizabeth accused King Richard of the crime. Even King Richard's wife, Anne, was found dead! Soon others rose against King Richard, and an army was created to defeat him. At the head of the army was Henry, Earl of Richmond, of the House of Lancaster.

Page Nine

Lord Rivers: Have patience, madam, his majesty will soon recover his accustomed health.

Stanley: We have just seen the king.

Buckingham: His majesty speaks cheerfully!

Queen Elizabeth: If he dies, what will become of me?

Grey: You have a goodly son, who will be your comforter.

Queen Elizabeth: Yes, but he is young, and would be in the care of Richard Gloucester, who loves no one here.

(Enter Gloucester, angrily.)

Gloucester: Who are they that complain to the king that I love them not?

Grey: To whom do you speak, your grace?

Gloucester: To thee, and thee! A plague on all of you!

Queen Elizabeth: You envy my advancement, and my friends. God grant that we never may have need of you.

Page Five

When Edward, Prince of Wales, who was only just a boy, arrived in London, he was greeted by his uncle, Richard. He was also greeted by his brother, young Richard, Duke of York. As King Edward had wished, Richard was made Lord Protector of the king, because Edward was so young. Richard decided that they should go to the Tower for safety, until it was time for the coronation.

The princes are glad to see each other. Portray them as kind, but honest in their understanding of their new positions.

Prince: How fares our loving brother?

York: Well, my dread lord, for so must I call you now.

Prince: Ay, brother, our grief is yours.

York: You have outgrown me far!

Gloucester: Please, my lord, you must now go to the Tower. Your mother will come and welcome you there.

Prince: Will you come, brother?

York: Yes, but I shall not sleep quietly in the Tower.

Page Eight

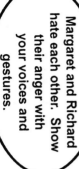

(Enter the old queen, Queen Margaret.)

Margaret and Richard hate each other. Show their anger with your voices and gestures.

Queen Margaret: *(To Gloucester.)* Out devil! You killed my husband, Henry, in the Tower, and my son at Tewksbury. You turn the sun to shade!

Gloucester: Have done, thou hateful, withered hag! Many of you were factious for the House of Lancaster, and I will not forget it!

As the others went to see the ailing King Edward, two murderers entered and crept close to Richard.

Gloucester: How now, my hardy, stout, resolved mates!

Murderer 1: We have come to have the warrant that we may be admitted to the Tower, where he is.

Page Six

Gloucester: *(Gives the paper.)* My brother Clarence is well spoken, and may move your hearts to pity, if you mark him.

Murderer 2: Fear not, we shall not turn from killing him.

In silence the two murderers left Richard's side, went to the Tower of London, and killed George, Duke of Clarence, in his cell. At the same time, King Edward was being visited by friends and family alike. When a messenger arrived to bring the sad news that Clarence was dead, the king's health grew worse, and he was rushed away to his bed. Soon after, King Edward died.

Queen Elizabeth: Who shall hinder me to wail and weep?

Duchess of York: What means this scene?

Queen Elizabeth: Edward, my lord and your son, our king, is dead.

Duchess of York: O sadness! First my son Clarence, now Edward!

After the king's death, while Richard waited for Edward, Prince of Wales to come to London, he began to get rid of some of his personal enemies. Rivers and Grey were sent to prison and executed at Pomfret Castle, just as Richard had threatened.

Page Seven

Julius Caesar

Performance Length	Number of Parts	Genre
10 to 15 Minutes	19	Tragedy

Synopsis

Long ago, in Rome, members of the senate were growing increasingly worried about the popularity of the great general, Julius Caesar. When Caesar is offered the emperor's crown, the rebellious senators act, some for political reasons, others out of their love for Rome and its institutions. They assassinate Julius Caesar on the Ides of March, as a soothsayer had predicted. Those loyal to Caesar, such as Marc Antony, raise an army to hunt down and bring the conspirators to justice. Eventually, all of the conspirators are caught and killed, although a few opt for suicide, such as Marcus Brutus, the "noblest Roman of them all". To restore order, Caesar's nephew, Octavius, agrees to rule Rome, as part of a triumvirate that also includes Marc Antony and M. Aemilius Lepidus.

Characters

Reading Levels of Difficulty

Non-Speaking (NS) **Easy (E)** **Moderate (M)** **Challenging (C)**

Julius Caesar **(M)** Marc Antony **(C)** Octavius **(M)**
M. Aemilius Lepidus **(NS)** Marcus Brutus **(C)** Cassius **(C)**
Casca **(M)** Cinna **(E)** Other Senators 3 **(NS)**
Calpurnia **(M)** Portia **(E)** Soothsayer **(E)**
Citizen 1 **(M)** Citizen 2 **(M)** Citizen 3 **(M)**
Clitus **(E)** Narrator **(M)**

Pronunciation Guide

Many of the names in this play are from ancient Rome.

Cinna (sin-na)   **Portia** (por-sha)   **Clitus** (clee-tus)

Staging & Costumes

Decorating the stage with some kind of bust in the style of a Roman leader would be effective, and would help establish the setting. A large sign with the letters SPQR (the Roman Republic and Empire) and the symbol of an eagle would also help establish the setting. The costumes can be kept very simple, as suggested in the costume section of the Teacher Guide at the beginning of this resource. To differentiate Caesar, he could be shown wearing a red sash draped diagonally across his chest.

Teaching Tips

- What was ancient Rome like? What were its laws? What were its customs? Look at buildings, art, pictures, etc., to give some background.
- Discuss what is meant by a tragedy.
- Discuss briefly the constant struggle for power in Rome between the Senate and the Emperor.
- Brainstorm ideas about "What is a hero?". Who is the hero in this play? Is there one?
- Discuss: Both Caesar and Brutus have tragic deaths. For whom do you feel most sorry? Why?

Extension Activities

- Retell the story of the assassination and campaign to bring the conspirators to justice as a newspaper article or as a TV news report, highlighting the brave deeds.
- Draw a picture of your favorite scene in the play/write a paragraph telling why you chose it.

Julius Caesar

Dramatis Personae

Julius Caesar — _____

Marc Antony — _____

Octavius — _____

M. Aemilius Lepidus — _____

Marcus Brutus — _____

Cassius — _____

Casca — _____

Cinna — _____

Other Senators (3) — _____

Calpurnia — _____

Portia — _____

Soothsayer — _____

Citizen 1 — _____

Citizen 2 — _____

Citizen 3 — _____

Clitus — _____

Narrator — _____

Page One

(Cries are heard approaching them.)

Clitus: Fly, my lord, fly!

(Exit all but Brutus.)

Brutus: Caesar, now be still. *(Falls on his sword.)*

(Enter Marc Antony, Octavius, and Lepidus.)

Marc Antony is truly saddened by Brutus' death. These words should be spoken in a solemn way.

Marc Antony: This was the noblest Roman of them all. He only, of all the conspirators, in a general honest thought, and common good to all, made one of them. His life was gentle, and the elements so mixed in him, that nature might stand up and say to all the world, "This was a man!"

Octavius: According to his virtue let us use him, with all respect and rites of burial. Within my tent his bones tonight shall lie, most like a soldier, ordered honorably. So call the field to rest, and let's away, to part the glories of this happy day!

Page Twelve

For many years in Rome, the Senate had been the voice of the people, a place where the city's leading citizens debated and passed the laws that governed the heart of Rome and her republic. However, several members of the Senate grew concerned over the military successes of Julius Caesar, and feared that he wanted even more power.

In a great procession, Julius Caesar entered the public square with his wife, Calpurnia, Marc Antony, Marcus Brutus and his wife, Portia, Cassius and several other senators, and a great crowd of citizens all celebrating Caesar's successes.

Julius Caesar: Set on, and leave no ceremony out.

Soothsayer: Caesar!

Julius Caesar: Ha! Who calls? I hear a voice shriller than all the music.

The soothsayer is a mysterious fortune teller. Everyone but Caesar should appear concerned by his words.

Page Two

Brutus: Why com'st thou?

Julius Caesar: To tell thee, thou shalt see me at Philippi.

Brutus: Why, I will see thee at Philippi then.

The next day, the conspirators fell one by one to the triumvirate's advancing army. During the fighting, Brutus and Cassius spoke in haste.

Cassius: If we lose this battle, are you contented to be led through the streets of Rome?

Brutus: No, Cassius, no. But this same day must end the work the Ides of March begun. And whether we shall meet again, I know not. Therefore our everlasting farewell take. If we do meet again, we shall smile. If not, why then, this parting was well made.

Cassius: Forever, and forever, farewell Brutus!

Brutus: As the battle wore on, Cassius took his own life in despair, and Brutus was left alone with some men loyal to him. Unwilling to be taken to Rome, and paraded as a prize before the citizens, Brutus decided to act.

Brutus: Farewell to you and you, and you. Night hangs upon mine eyes, my bones would rest, that have but labored to attain this hour.

Page Eleven

Soothsayer:	Beware the Ides of March.
Julius Caesar:	What man is that?
Brutus:	A soothsayer, a man who foretells the future, bids you beware the Ides of March.
Julius Caesar:	Set him before me. Let me see his face.
Cassius:	Fellow, look upon Caesar.
Julius Caesar:	What sayest thou to me now? Speak once again.
Soothsayer:	Beware the Ides of March.
Julius Caesar:	He is a dreamer; let us leave him. Pass.
(Exit all but Cassius and Brutus.)	
Cassius:	Can you see your face, Brutus?
Brutus:	No, Cassius, for the eye sees not itself, but by reflection by some other things.
Cassius:	You look very troubled of late.
(A loud cheer is heard.)	
Brutus:	What means this shouting? O, I do fear the people choose Caesar for their king.

Page Three

Citizen 3:	We will be revenged! Seek! Burn! Kill! Slay! Let not a traitor live!
Citizens:	Take up his body! Revenge! *(Exit Citizens.)*
Marc Antony:	*(To the audience.)* Now let it work. Mischief, thou art afoot!

After Marc Antony's speech, the citizens of Rome set about burning the homes of the traitorous senators. The conspirators fled together, and set up a camp near Sardis, with soldiers loyal to them. Inside Brutus' tent, they met to discuss their plans. Brutus and Cassius argued, and the sad news that Portia, Brutus' wife, had died, was delivered. Against some of the conspirator's advice, they decided to meet an army commanded by Marc Antony, Octavius, and Lepidus, who had come together to rule Rome in Caesar's place. They would battle at a place called Philippi.

Later that night, on the eve of battle, Brutus sat alone in his tent, tiredly trying to read by a candle's dying light.

(Enter the ghost of Caesar.)

Brutus:	Ha! Who comes here? Monstrous apparition, it comes upon me! Speak to me what thou art!
Julius Caesar:	Thy evil spirit, Brutus.

Page Ten

Cassius: Do you fear it? Then must I think you would not have it so.

Brutus: I would not, yet I love him well. But why do you hold me here so long?

Cassius: I was born free of Caesar, and so were you, but this man is now become a god. He doth bestride the narrow world like a Colossus, and we petty men walk under his legs and peep about. How can Rome be a place where there is in it but one only man?

Brutus: What has happened, Casca? Why the shouting?

Casca: Three times was Caesar offered the crown of Rome by Marc Antony, but he refused it each time.

Brutus: And after that, he came, thus sad, away?

Casca: Ay.

Brutus: What you have said, I will consider. Tomorrow, if you please to speak with me, I will come to your house.

Page Four

Citizens: Live, Brutus, live!

Citizen 1: Wait, let us hear Marc Antony!

Citizen 2: What does he say of Brutus?

Citizen 3: Let him speak!

Marc Antony: Friends, Romans, countrymen, lend me your ears. I come to bury Caesar, not to praise him. The evil that men do lives after them; the good is oft interred with their bones. So let it be with Caesar. Brutus says that Caesar was ambitious, but did he not thrice refuse the crown I presented him? Was this ambition? Bear with me. My heart is in the coffin there with Caesar, and I must pause till it come back to me.

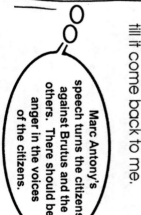

Marc Antony's speech turns the citizens against Brutus and the others. There should be anger in the voices of the citizens.

Citizen 1: They were traitors!

Citizen 2: They were villains!

Marc Antony: Brutus was Caesar's angel. This was the most unkindest cut of all, and burst his mighty heart.

Page Nine

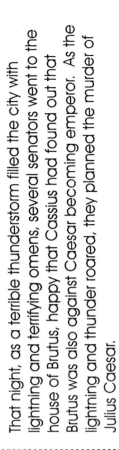

That night, as a terrible thunderstorm filled the city with lightning and terrifying omens, several senators went to the house of Brutus, happy that Cassius had found out that Brutus was also against Caesar becoming emperor. As the lightning and thunder roared, they planned the murder of Julius Caesar.

Cassius: Good morrow, Brutus. Do we trouble you?

Brutus does what he thinks is best for Rome. This decision has been very difficult for him.

Brutus: I have been awake all night, and I know why you have come. We all stand up against the spirit of Caesar. Give me your hands all over, one by one.

Cassius: Should Marc Antony fall with Caesar?

Brutus: No, our course will seem too bloody. Let us part for now, and let not our looks put on our purposes. *(Exit all. Enter Portia, Brutus' wife.)* Portia, what mean you? Wherefore rise you now?

Page Five

Brutus: You shall, Marc Antony. Take you Caesar's body, and you shall not in your funeral speech blame us.

(Exit conspirators.)

Marc Antony: *(To Caesar's body.)* O, pardon me that I am meek and gentle with these butchers! Thou art the ruins of the noblest man that ever lived in the tide of times. Woe to the hand that shed this costly blood! Caesar's spirit shall, with a monarch's voice, cry "Havoc!", and let slip the dogs of war!

Later, in the Forum, before the citizens of Rome, Brutus told them why the senators had killed Julius Caesar.

Citizen 1: We will be satisfied!

Citizen 2: I will hear Brutus speak.

Citizen 3: The noble Brutus speaks. Silence!

Brutus: Romans, countrymen! Hear me for my cause! No one loved Caesar more than I, but I loved Rome more! As Caesar was ambitious, I slew him. I give him honor for his valor, but death for his ambition. I slew him for the good of Rome, and I have kept the same dagger for myself.

Page Eight

OTM-1867 • SSR1-67 Shakespeare Shorts

Portia: What is happening? I should know this secret.

Brutus: I shall tell you, by and by.

The next day was the ides of March. As Caesar prepared to go to the Senate, Calpurnia, his wife, begged him not to go.

Calpurnia: You shall not stir out of your house today. Last night's storm foretold terrible things. A lioness whelped in the streets, graves opened and yielded up their dead, and ghosts did shriek and squeal about the streets. I do fear these things!

Julius Caesar: Cowards die many times before their deaths; the valiant never taste death but once. Caesar shall forth.

At the Senate, the eight conspirators were ready, and all concealed daggers in their clothing. To ensure their success, Marc Antony was called out of the Senate chamber so he could not help Caesar. When the time was right, they surrounded Caesar and each stabbed with his dagger. Under the weight of their blows, Caesar staggered and fell.

Casca: Speak, hands for me!

Page Six

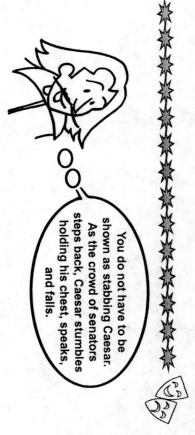

You do not have to be shown as stabbing Caesar. As the crowd of senators steps back, Caesar stumbles holding his chest, speaks, and falls.

(All surround Caesar, then step back.)

Julius Caesar: Et tu, Brute? Then fall, Caesar! *(He falls and dies.)*

Cinna: Liberty! Freedom! Tyranny is dead! Run hence, proclaim, cry it about the streets!

(Enter Marc Antony.)

Brutus: Here comes Marc Antony.

Marc Antony: O, mighty Caesar! Dost thou lie so low? Fare thee well.

Brutus: *(To Marc Antony.)* You see but what our hands have done; our hearts you see not. They are pitiful, and pity to the general wrong of Rome hath done this deed on Caesar.

Marc Antony: May I speak at his funeral?

Page Seven

Romeo and Juliet

Performance Length	Number of Parts	Genre
15 to 20 Minutes	23	Tragedy

Synopsis

The Montague and Capulet families have been feuding, threatening the peace of Verona, so the Prince promises banishment to anyone who breaks the peace. At a masquerade ball, Romeo and Juliet see each other and fall in love; later they plan marriage. With the help of Friar Laurence, their plan begins, but it goes horribly wrong when Romeo does not receive an important message, and thinking Juliet dead, he kills himself. Waking beside the dead Romeo, Juliet also takes her own life. Their families arrive too late, and the tragedy of their children forces peace on the families.

Characters

Reading Levels of Difficulty:

Non-Speaking (NS)	Easy (E)	Moderate (M)	Challenging (C)

Romeo **(C)**	Juliet **(C)**	Escalus, Prince of Verona **(M)**
Juliet's Nurse **(C)**	Mercutio **(M)**	Tybalt **(C)**
Friar Laurence **(C)**	A Capulet Man **(E)**	Benvolio **(E)**
Balthasar **(E)**	A Montague Man **(NS)**	Romeo's Father **(E)**
Romeo's Mother **(NS)**	Apothecary **(NS)**	Juliet's Father **(C)**
Juliet's Mother **(M)**	Citizens of Verona (4) **(E)**	Escalus' soldiers (2) **(NS)**
Narrator **(M)**		

Pronunciation Guide

Mercutio (mer-cue'-she-oh)   **Tybalt** (tibb'-alt)

Staging & Costumes

The staging can be accomplished very simply. Limited props: Juliet will need something to sleep on, perhaps some gym mats, stacked four or five high, covered by a floral shower curtain or other fabric. Weapons are mimed. Costumes are similar to other play suggestions (see page 7 of the Teacher Guide).

Teaching Tips

• Discuss conflict; what harm can it do? Brainstorm ideas. Relate it to this play.
• Discuss *Romeo and Juliet* as one of the most famous and plays ever written. What is the students' background knowledge? Chart it and see how it compares with the actual play.

Extension Activities

• Draw a picture of your favorite scene in the play and write a paragraph telling why you chose it.
• Write a newspaper article chronicling the events in the play, or an editorial on the harmful effects of violence, using examples from the play.
• Violence between families played a part the deaths of Romeo and Juliet. How has violence affected your community, or those of others around the country and the world? Discuss.

Romeo And Juliet

Dramatis Personae

Romeo –

Juliet –

Escalus, Prince of Verona –

Juliet's Nurse –

Mercutio –

Tybalt –

Friar Laurence –

A Capulet Man –

Benvolio –

A Montague Man –

Romeo's Father –

Romeo's Mother –

Juliet's Father –

Juliet's Mother –

Citizens of Verona (4) –

Escalus' soldiers (2) –

Balthasar –

Apothecary –

Narrator –

Page One

Prince: *(Reads the letter.)* This letter doth make good the friar's words, their course of love, the tidings of her death, and how he came to lie in this tomb. *(Angry.)* Capulet! Montague! See what a scourge is laid upon your hate! Both families must now end their fight. Look what it has done!

Capulet: O, brother Montague, give me thy hand.

Montague: I can give thee more. I will raise a statue in gold of true and faithful Juliet.

As the Prince speaks, all others bow their heads in sorrow. Pronunciation note: Say "pun-ish-ed" in this speech to make it rhyme.

Prince: A glooming peace this morning with it brings;
The sun, for sorrow, will not show his head:
Go hence, to have more talk of these sad things;
Some shall be pardon'd, and some punished;
For never was a story of more woe,
Than this of Juliet and her Romeo.

Page Sixteen

Two households, both alike in dignity, in fair Verona, have been fighting for years. The Montagues and the Capulets have had many fights, and many good people have died or have been saddened. The Prince and the people of Verona have had enough.

(Enter Capulet Man and Montague Man, *fighting with swords. Enter Benvolio.*)

Benvolio: Part, fools! Put up your swords, you know not what you do.

(Enter Tybalt.)

Tybalt: Turn thee, Benvolio, look upon thy death.

(Enter citizens.)

Citizens: Down with the Capulets! Down with the Montagues!

(Enter Escalus, *Prince of Verona, with soldiers.*)

Prince: Rebellious subjects, enemies to peace, listen to me. Stop your fighting! If you fight again, you will have to answer to me and the law! Now, all men, on pain of death, depart!

Page Two

Too late, both families entered with Friar Laurence, Balthasar, and the Prince.

Prince: What misadventure is so early up, that calls me from my morning rest?

Lady Capulet: The people in the street cry Romeo – some Juliet; and all run, with open outcry, toward our monument.

Prince: What fear is this?

Capulet: O, Heaven! Look at our daughter! Look at Romeo!

Prince: What dost thou know in this?

Friar Laurence: What has happened here? Both dead?

Friar Laurence: Romeo was husband to Juliet. After Tybalt was killed, I gave her a sleeping potion, so that they could meet. But the letter that I sent to Romeo to tell him of my plan, could not be delivered. And now I find them both dead.

Prince: What can you say to this?

Balthasar: I have a letter from Romeo that he early bid me give his father.

Page Fifteen

The two families left quietly, staring at each other.

As Benvolio left, he met his kinsman, Romeo, of the Montague house, who seemed sad. He was sad because the girl he loved, named Rosaline, did not love him in return. To cheer up Romeo, Benvolio invited him to sneak with him, in disguise, to old Capulet's house for a masquerade ball. Benvolio joked that Romeo would probably see a girl there even more beautiful than Rosaline. Even though it was dangerous, Romeo agreed, and so, that night, Romeo, Benvolio, and their best friend, Mercutio, sneaked into the house of their enemy.

At the ball, Romeo saw Juliet and fell in love with her.

Romeo: What lady's that? O, she doth teach the torches to burn bright! Did my heart love till now? Forswear it, sight! For I never saw true beauty till this night.

While Romeo admired Juliet from across the room, he was seen by Tybalt, Juliet's cousin, who was watching from a distance with Juliet's father.

Romeo should be portrayed as polite, kind, and honest, while Tybalt should be shown to be angry and ready to fight at a moment's notice.

Page Three

Unfortunately, Friar Laurence had sent a letter to tell Romeo about the plan, but he didn't receive it, because the man who was supposed to deliver it could not. When he realized the danger, Friar Laurence raced to Juliet's tomb, hoping to keep her safe until Romeo arrived. However, Romeo reached the tomb before Friar Laurence, and thinking that Juliet was dead, he was very sad.

Romeo: Oh, my love! Death, that hath sucked the honey of thy breath hath no power yet upon thy beauty. Here, here will I remain. O, here will I set up my everlasting rest. Here's to my love! *(Drinks the poison.)* O true, apothecary! Thy drugs are quick. And so I die. Eyes look your last!

(Romeo dies. After a moment's silent pause, Juliet wakes.)

The pause must be done carefully, not too long, not too short. It allows the audience time to take in what Romeo's actions mean to both he and Juliet.

Juliet: Where is my lord? Where is my Romeo? *(Sees Romeo and gasps.)* What's here? A cup, closed in my true love's hand. Poison, I see, and no friendly drop to help me after. *(Takes Romeo's dagger and stabs herself.)* O happy dagger! This is thy sheath, and let me die. *(She falls dead.)*

Page Fourteen

Tybalt: This, by his voice, should be a Montague. To strike him dead I hold it not a sin.

Capulet: Why are you angry, kinsman?

Tybalt: Uncle, this is a Montague, our foe, 'Tis he, that villain Romeo.

Capulet: Let him alone. Verona brags of him to be a well-governed youth.

Tybalt: I'll not endure him!

Capulet: He shall be endured. Am I not the master here? Be quiet, for shame! Or I'll make you quiet.

When Juliet noticed Romeo during a dance, she fell in love with him.

Juliet: Nurse, who is he? Go, ask his name.

Nurse: His name is Romeo, and a Montague, the only son of your great enemy.

Juliet: Oh! My only love sprung from my only hate.

Page Four

So Juliet drank the potion and fell asleep, and her family thought she was dead.

Juliet: What if this mixture does not work at all? How if, when I am laid in the tomb, I wake before the time that Romeo comes to redeem me? Alack, alack! Romeo, I come! This do I drink to thee. *(She falls on the bed.)*

(Enter Nurse.)

Nurse: Alas! Alas! Help, help! My lady's dead!

(Enter Capulet and Lady Capulet.)

Lady Capulet: What noise is here? O me, O me! My child! Alack the day!

Capulet: Alas, she's cold! Death, that hath taken her hence to make me wail, ties up my tongue, and will not let me speak.

Juliet's family was very sad, and laid her in the tomb.

Meanwhile, in Mantua, Romeo met a servant from the Montague's house called Balthasar, who brought the sad news that Juliet was dead. Romeo was shocked, and being distraught, bought a deadly poison from an apothecary, a man of medicine, and headed back to Verona.

Page Thirteen

Friar Laurence: Romeo will come to her. I have a plan. Romeo, go hence, and stay in Mantua. I'll send you news of my plan. Give me thy hand; farewell; good night.

Before leaving Verona, Romeo rushed to see Juliet in secret. They talked while Juliet's nurse kept watch.

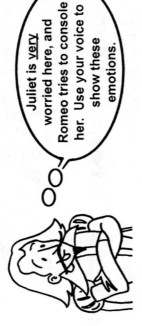

Juliet is _very_ worried here, and **Romeo tries to console her. Use your voice to show these emotions.**

Juliet: Wilt thou be gone?

Romeo: I must be gone and live, or stay and die. Farewell!

Juliet: O, thinkest thou we shall ever meet again?

Romeo: I doubt it not! Adieu! Adieu!

Soon after, Juliet went to see Friar Laurence. He told her of his plan. He gave Juliet a potion that would make her seem like she was dead, when she was only sleeping. After her family put her in the family tomb in the church, she would wake up and leave Verona to meet Romeo.

Page Twelve

Later that night, after the party was over, Romeo left his friends, and sneaked back to Juliet's house. There, he saw her on her balcony.

Benvolio: *(Whispering.)* Romeo! My cousin Romeo! Where are you?

Mercutio: He is wise, and has gone home to bed.

Benvolio: He ran this way, and leaped this orchard wall. Call, good Mercutio.

Mercutio: Nay, I won't. Romeo, good night. Come, Benvolio, it is too cold for me here now.

(Exit Benvolio and Mercutio. Enter Romeo, seeing Juliet come out on her balcony.)

This is one of the most famous scenes ever written. **Be sure that you know your lines, and that you show the joy they both have in being together.**

Romeo: But soft, what light through yonder window breaks?
It is the east, and Juliet is the sun.
It is my lady; O, it is my love.

Page Five

Juliet: *(Sighing.)* Ay, me.

Romeo: She speaks! O, speak again!

Juliet: O, Romeo, Romeo, wherefore art thou, Romeo?
Deny thy father, and refuse your name.
O, be some other name! What's in a name?
That which we call a rose, by any other name
would smell as sweet.

Romeo: *(Stepping out into the open.)*
I take thee at thy word.

Juliet: What man art thou, thus bescreened in night?

Romeo: I know not how to tell thee who I am.

Juliet: Art thou not Romeo? How cam'st thou hither?

Romeo: With love's light wings did I o'er-perch these walls.

Juliet: If my kinsmen do see thee, they will murder thee.

Romeo: Alack! There lies more peril in thine eye,
Than in twenty of their swords.

Juliet: Dost thou love me? I know, thou wilt say – Ay;
And I will take thy word.

Romeo: I wish the exchange of thy love's faithful vow
for mine.

Page Six

Citizens: Call for the prince!

Prince: Where are the vile beginners of this fray?
Who killed Tybalt?

Capulet Man: Romeo did!

Prince: For that offence, immediately do we exile
him hence. He can never return to Verona!

Romeo ran to Friar Laurence, and told him what had
happened. Friar Laurence told him to leave town, because
he had an idea to help. Unfortunately, he did not tell Romeo
his plans because there wasn't enough time.

Friar Laurence: Romeo, come hence. Here from Verona
art thou banished. *(A knocking is heard.)*
Good Romeo, hide thyself.

Friar Laurence: Who's there?

(Enter Juliet's nurse.)

Friar Laurence: Welcome then.

Romeo: Nurse! How is Juliet?

Nurse: O, she says nothing, but weeps and weeps.

Page Eleven

Juliet: I gave thee mine before thou didst request it. My love is as deep as the sea.

They talked for a while longer and decided to get married, even though it would make their parents angry.

Romeo: O blessed, blessed night! I am afraid all this is but a dream.

Juliet: Send me word tomorrow when I should come to thee, where and when we shall be married. Good night, good night! A thousand times good night! Parting is such sweet sorrow!

After he left, Romeo went to see his friend Friar Laurence to tell him about Juliet and their plans. Friar Laurence was happy for Romeo, but worried too because Romeo was a Montague, and Juliet was a Capulet.

Romeo: Good morrow, father!

Friar Laurence: What early tongue so sweet saluteth me? Is it Romeo?

Romeo: I am in love, father.

Page Seven

Tybalt: *(To Mercutio. Draws his sword as well.)* What would'st thou have with me? I am for you.

(They fight with swords.)

Romeo: Gentle Mercutio, put thy rapier up.

Suddenly, Mercutio was stabbed because Romeo had tried to stop him. His friends didn't think he was badly hurt, but he soon died of the wound.

Mercutio: I am hurt.

Romeo: Courage man, the hurt cannot be much.

Mercutio: Why the devil came you between us?

Romeo: I thought all for the best.

Mercutio: O, I die, Romeo! A plague on both your houses!

Romeo was shocked that his friend was dead. He grew very angry, and chased and killed Tybalt in a sword fight. Realizing what he had done, Romeo ran away in fear.

Benvolio: Romeo, away, begone! The citizens are up, and Tybalt slain. Hence! Begone! Away!

Page Ten

48

Friar Laurence: (laughing.) With Rosaline?

Romeo: I have forgot that name. I love Juliet, the fair daughter of rich Capulet. Will you marry us?

Friar Laurence: This alliance may so happy prove, To turn your households' rancor to pure love.

Romeo: Hurry! I stand on sudden haste!

Friar Laurence: Wisely, and slow; they stumble, that run fast.

The next day, Juliet's nurse received a message from him, and she brought Juliet to meet Friar Laurence and Romeo. They were married that evening in Friar Laurence's room.

Friar Laurence: Here comes the lady, O, so light a foot.

Juliet: Good evening, Friar.

Romeo: Juliet, my joy is too great.

Juliet: My true love has grown to excess.

Friar Laurence: Come, come with me, and be married.

Page Eight

On his way home, alone, after the wedding, Romeo met Mercutio and Benvolio, arguing with Tybalt and the Capulet gang.

This scene changes the play from a romance to a tragedy. Romeo's actions begin a chain of events that will eventually lead to the tragic ending of the play.

Benvolio: By my heel, here come the Capulets.

(Enter citizens, watching.)

Mercutio: (Angrily.) Consort! 'Zounds, consort!

Tybalt: Mercutio, thou consort'st with Romeo.

Benvolio: Either speak in private, Tybalt, or else depart. Here all eyes gaze on us.

(Enter Romeo.)

Tybalt: Here comes my man. Romeo, thou art a villain.

Romeo: I do protest, I never injured thee.

(Mercutio draws his sword.)

Page Nine

Macbeth

Performance Length	Number of Parts	Genre
20 to 25 Minutes	24	Tragedy

Synopsis

Once upon a time, in the kingdom of Scotland, Macbeth and his ambitious wife plot to take the throne by assassinating the king, Duncan. Once Macbeth is crowned king, their remorse and guilt cause them both to hallucinate. Their strange behavior raises suspicions among the Scottish Lords, who raise an army, kill Macbeth, and place King Duncan's son, Malcolm, on the throne.

Characters

Reading Levels of Difficulty:
Non-Speaking (NS)   Easy (E)   Moderate (M)   Challenging (C)

Macbeth **(C)**	Banquo and Banquo's Ghost **(M)**	Lady Macbeth **(C)**
King Duncan **(M)**	Malcolm, Duncan's son **(E)**	Donalbain, Duncan's son **(E)**
Macduff **(M)**	Lennox **(M)**	Ross **(M)**
Angus **(E)**	Scottish Lords (2) **(E)**	The Three Witches **(C)**
Apparition **(E)**	Murderer 1 **(E)**	Murderer 2 **(E)**
Captain **(M)**	Fleance, Banquo's son **(E)**	King Duncan's Guards (2) **(NS)**
Attendant **(E)**	Narrator **(M)**	

Pronunciation Guide

Banquo (bank'-kwo)   **Malcolm** (mal'-come)   **Fleance** (flay'-ahnce)
Donalbain (don-al'-bin)

Staging & Costumes

The staging can be accomplished very simply. A toy cauldron, or a cardboard cut out might be a nice touch for the witches. As the army of the Scottish Lords comes out, have the students carry imitation tree branches in front of their faces, dropping them before the battle, miming the realization of the prophesy made by the witches of Birnam Wood coming to Dunsinane.

As far as costumes, a crown will have to be made. The ghost of Banquo might use a mask, or a flashlight to illuminate its face. The witches can be created effectively with simple black clothes and pointy witch hats.

Teaching Tips

• Discuss what is meant by greed, ambition, revenge, and remorse. Relate these to the play.

Extension Activities

• Compare the witches in this story with those in other stories (How are they similar? Different?)
• A discussion point: Why did Macbeth believe the witches? Did they only say what he wanted to hear? Or did they have a hand in his tragic end?
• Design a mask showing one of the characters in the play.
• Find Scotland on a map.
• Draw a picture of your favorite scene in the play and write a paragraph telling why you chose it.

Macbeth

Dramatis Personae

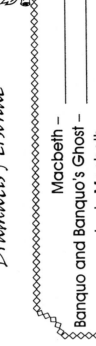

Macbeth –

Banquo and Banquo's Ghost –

Lady Macbeth –

King Duncan –

Malcolm, Duncan's son –

Donalbain, Duncan's son –

Macduff –

Lennox –

Ross –

Angus –

Scottish Lords (2) –

Witch 1 –

Witch 2 –

Witch 3 –

Apparition –

Murderer 1 –

Murderer 2 –

King Duncan's Guards (2) –

Fleance, Banquo's son –

Captain –

Attendant –

Narrator –

Page One

Macduff: Yield thee, coward.

Macbeth: I will not yield.

Finally, Macduff killed Macbeth, took his crown, and returned to tell Malcolm the news. When the Scottish lords realized that Macbeth was dead, Malcolm was proclaimed King of Scotland, and he gave the title of Earl to his loyal nobles. Peace had come to Scotland again.

Macduff: *(Places the crown on Malcolm's head.)* Hail, King! For so thou art. Hail King of Scotland!

Malcolm: May thanes and kinsmen, henceforth be earls. So thanks to all at once, and to each one, whom we invite to see us crowned king.

Scottish Lords: Hail, Malcolm, King of Scotland!

Page Twenty

As Scotland is threatened by an army from Norway, supported by Scottish traitors, strange things begin to happen. As Duncan, King of Scotland, prepares to honor his general, Macbeth, for his bravery in battle, three witches also plan to greet Macbeth with an eerie prophecy.

The witches should be hunched and mysterious.

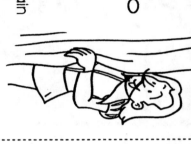

Witch 1: When shall we three meet again
In thunder, lightning, or in rain?

Witch 2: When the hurly-burly's done,
When the battle's lost and won.

Witch 3: That will be ere the set of sun.

Witch 2: Upon the heath.

Witch 3: There to meet with Macbeth.

Witches: Fair is foul, and foul is fair;
Hover through the fog and filthy air.

Page Two

Macbeth: Out, out, brief candle! Life's but a walking shadow, a poor player that struts and frets his hour upon the stage and then is heard no more. It is a tale told by an idiot, full of sound and fury, signifying nothing.

Attendant: I should report what else I saw. As I did stand upon the hill, I looked toward Birnham, and anon, methought the wood began to move.

Macbeth: Liar! Arm, arm, and out! Ring the alarm-bell! Now we go to battle! Blow wind! Come, wrack!

Soon Macbeth saw that what the attendant had said was true. The opposing army had cut branches from the trees of Birnham Wood, and carried the branches before them to hide their numbers.

On the battlefield, Macbeth met an army that included Malcolm, dead King Duncan's son, Macduff, and the other Scottish lords. They wanted revenge for the things that Macbeth had done.

(Enter Malcolm, Macduff, and two Scottish lords, holding tree branches in front of their faces to hide their numbers.)

On the battlefield, Macbeth met Macduff, and they had a terrible sword fight.

Page Nineteen

Meanwhile, in the king's camp near the battlefield, news of Macbeth's bravery and skills arrives yet again.

Duncan: What bloody man is that?

Malcolm: A sergeant who fought for my freedom, father. Hail, brave friend. Tell the king of your news.

Captain: Brave Macbeth, disdaining Fortune, has slain the traitor, Macdonald, who had joined with Norway. But then the Norwegian lord began a fresh attack.

Duncan: Were Macbeth and Banquo dismayed?

Captain: No, they redoubled their strokes on the foe.

(Enter Ross.)

Ross: God save the king! Norway, and the traitorous thane of Cawdor are beaten. Victory has fallen to us!

Duncan: We will grant Macbeth the thane of Cawdor's title as a reward for his bravery. What Cawdor hath lost, Macbeth hath won.

Page Three

Lady Macbeth: Yet here's a spot! Out, cursed spot! Out, I say! Here's the smell of blood still. Oh! Oh! Oh! I cannot wash it away. What's done cannot be undone.

When Macbeth returned, he saw the Scottish lords' army massing against him. However, just before the battle, an attendant told Macbeth that his wife was dead, and some other troubling news.

[The cry of a woman is heard.]

Macbeth: Wherefore was that cry?

Attendant: The Queen, my lord, is dead.

Macbeth's response to the news of his wife's death shows that he is losing hope. He thinks that life seems too meaningless when he says that it signifies nothing, and that everything he has done, both good and bad, will amount to nothing.

Page Eighteen

While riding home from their victory in battle, Macbeth and his friend Banquo met the three witches standing on the heath.

Macbeth: A drum, a drum! Macbeth doth come!

Witches: So foul and fair a day I have not seen.

Banquo: What are these? So withered, and so wild in their attire. Are they witches?

Macbeth: Speak, if you can. What are you?

Witch 1: All hail, Macbeth, Thane of Glamis!

Witch 2: All hail, Macbeth, Thane of Cawdor!

Witch 3: All hail, Macbeth, thou shalt be king hereafter!

Banquo: Good sir, why do you start and seem to fear things that do sound so fair? What of me, witches? Speak, then to me.

Witches: Hail!

Witch 1: Lesser than Macbeth, and greater!

Witch 2: Not so happy, yet much happier!

Witch 2: Demand.

Witch 3: We'll answer.

Macbeth: What will happen to me?

An apparition rose slowly form the cauldron and answered Macbeth's question.

> The apparition should be slow moving and very eerie.

Macbeth: That will never be!

Apparition: Macbeth shall never vanquished be, until Birnham Wood to high Dunsinane hill shall come against him.

Meanwhile, back at her castle, Lady Macbeth began to feel very guilty for having her king and Banquo killed. She also began to feel nervous that the Scottish lords were arming against her husband. She began wiping her hands again and again, imagining that she had blood on her hands.

OTM-1867 • SSR1-67 Shakespeare Shorts

Witch 3: All hail, Banquo, the father of kings!!

Macbeth: Stay and tell me more! What do you mean? I am already the Thane of Glamis, but another man is Thane of Cawdor. Say from whence you owe this strange intelligence. Speak, I charge you.

[The witches vanish.]

Banquo: Whither are they vanished?

Macbeth: Into the air, melted as breath into wind. *(Pauses.)* Your children shall be kings.

Banquo: You shall be king.

Macbeth: And thane of Cawdor too, went it not so?

(Enter Ross and Angus.)

Ross: Hail, Macbeth. The king hath happily received the news of thy success.

Angus: We are sent to give thee thanks, from our royal master.

Ross: And call thee thane of Cawdor!

Page Five

After Macbeth had gone, the Scottish lords began to suspect that he had killed his friend and king, and they prepared to fight against him. Macbeth, desperate to know what the future held for him, ran to find the three witches. He found them chanting and making a potion around a cauldron.

This is a very famous scene, with many famous lines. The witches should know their lines quite well, and be able to inject some eeriness and mystery into their actions and their voices.

Witches: Double, double, toil and trouble;
Fire burn, and cauldron bubble.
Fillet of a fenny snake,
In the cauldron boil and bake;
Eye of newt, and toe of frog,
Wool of bat, and tongue of dog.
For a charm of powerful trouble,
Double, double, toil and trouble,
Fire burn, and cauldron bubble.

Witch 1: By the pricking of my thumbs,
Something wicked this way comes.

Macbeth: Answer me to what I ask you.

Page Sixteen

OTM-1867 • SSR1-67 Shakespeare Shorts

Banquo: *(Aside, to himself and the audience.)*
What? Did the witches speak true?

Macbeth: Thanks for your pains.
(Aside, to himself and the audience.)
Two truths are told, as happy prologues
to the swelling act. The witches' words
cannot be ill; cannot be good. If
chance will have me king,
why, chance may crown me.

Macbeth shows his ambitions here, yet he is not so ambitious that he cannot wait for fate to bring the crown to him.

Macbeth's amazement that what the witches had said had come true made him begin to think about becoming king. He told his wife about it in a letter.

Lady Macbeth: *(Reading the letter.)*
The witches said, "Hail, thou shalt be king hereafter!" This I have thought good to deliver thee, my dearest partner of greatness. Lay it to thy heart.

Page Six

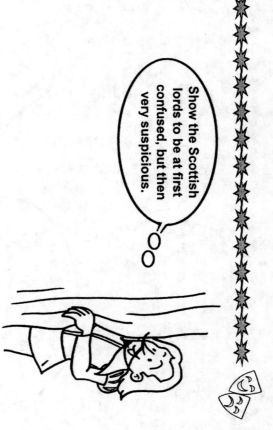

Show the Scottish lords to be at first confused, but then very suspicious.

Macbeth: *(To the ghost of Banquo.)*
Thou canst not say I did it!
Never shake thy gory locks at me!

Lady Macbeth: Why do you make such faces? You look but on a stool.

Ross: Gentlemen, rise, his highness is not well!

Macbeth: *(To the ghost.)*
Avaunt! And quit my sight!
Thy blood is cold!
Hence horrible shadow!
You have displaced the mirth!
Come with me, my lord. A kind good night to all.

Lennox: Good night, and better health attend his majesty.

Page Fifteen

Glamis thou art, and Cawdor. So, the three witches promised this to you. Then, my husband, you will become king too. I have a plan.

Lady Macbeth is very ambitious, and will even plan a murder to help her husband.

(Enter attendant.)

Attendant: My lady, the king comes here tonight with your husband. *(Exits.)*

Lady Macbeth: He brings great news. Come, thick night, and hide my evil plans in the dunnest smoke.

Now that Lady Macbeth knew that King Duncan was coming to visit their castle that very day, she made a plan to kill the king. As Duncan arrived, she told Macbeth about it. Later that night, Macbeth would sneak into Duncan's room, past his sleeping guards, and stab him to death. Then he would creep back to his room.

Page Seven

Murderer 1: Yes, my lord.

Macbeth: So is he mine now. I need your help.

Murderer 2: We shall, my lord, perform what you command us.

In the struggle with the murderers, Banquo was killed, but his son, Fleance, escaped. Rather than make him feel at peace, this news from the murderers, and his murder of King Duncan, made Macbeth feel nervous, and he started to see things.

At a dinner later that day, he saw the ghost of Banquo sitting at the table in his place. No one else could see the ghost. Lady Macbeth had to hurry Macbeth from the room.

Scottish Lords: Welcome, your majesty!

Lennox: May it please your highness to sit?

Macbeth: Where? The table's full.

Lennox: Here is a place reserved, sir.

Macbeth: *(Pointing at the chair where he sees the ghost of Banquo.)* Who is this? Which of you has done this?

Scottish Lords: What, my good lord?

Page Fourteen

That night, after a feast in his honor, King Duncan retired to his room.

Lady Macbeth: Now that he has gone to bed, let us talk. Are you ready to kill him?

Macbeth: If it were done when 'tis done, then 'twere well it were done quickly.

Lady Macbeth: Are you afraid to do what you desire? You will be king!

Macbeth: If we should fail?

Lady Macbeth: We fail! But be brave, and we'll not fail! When Duncan is asleep, I will give his two guards wine to drink, and they will fall into swinish sleep. What cannot you and I perform on the unguarded Duncan?

Macbeth: I am settled to this terrible feat. A false face must hide what the false heart doth know.

Late that night, as Macbeth headed to Duncan's room, he met Banquo with his son, Fleance.

Banquo: How goes the night, boy?

Page Eight

(Enter Macbeth and Lennox.)

Macbeth: Repent me of my fury, but I did kill them.

Macbeth kills the guards to hide the truth, but their deaths are too rash and too convenient, and eventually draws Banquo's suspicion to him. To draw attention away from Macbeth's actions, Lady Macbeth pretends to faint.

Lady Macbeth: Help me hence, ho! *(She pretends to faint.)*

Macduff: Look to the lady! And then let us meet and question this bloody piece of work.

In fear, King Duncan's sons fled Macbeth's castle, and this made some suspicious that they had committed the murder. But Banquo, who knew of the three witches' prophecy, suspected that Macbeth was guilty, especially when Macbeth was soon crowned king by the Scottish lords.

Recognizing his friend's suspicions, Macbeth hired two murderers to kill his friend, Banquo.

Macbeth: Both of you know Banquo, your enemy?

Page Thirteen

OTM-1867 • SSR1-67 Shakespeare Shorts

Fleance: The moon is down.

Banquo: Who's there?

(Enter Macbeth.)

Macbeth: A friend.

Banquo: All's well. I dreamt last night of the three witches. What they said to you has some truth.

Macbeth: I think not of them. You and your son should now go to bed. Good repose, the while!

Banquo: Thanks sir; the like to you!

As Banquo and Fleance left, Macbeth had a vision of a knife in the air before him.

Macbeth: Is this a dagger I see before me, the handle toward my hand. Come, let me clutch thee; I have thee not, and yet I see thee still, fatal vision, dagger of the mind. I go now, and it is done.

Page Nine

Macbeth and Lennox: What's the matter?

Macduff: The king is murdered! Murder and treason! *(Exit Macbeth and Lennox, to see the king.)* Banquo! Malcolm! Donalbain! Awake! Up, up, and see! Ring the bell!

(Enter Lady Macbeth, followed by Banquo.)

Lady Macbeth: What's this business?

Macduff: O, Banquo, Banquo, our royal master's murdered!

Lady Macbeth: Woe, alas! What, in our house?

Banquo: Too cruel anywhere!

(Enter Malcolm and Donalbain.)

Malcolm and Donalbain: What is amiss?

Macduff: You royal father's murdered!

Malcolm: O, by whom?

Macduff: His guards! Their hands and faces were all badged with blood. So were their daggers.

Page Twelve

Waiting for Macbeth to return, Lady Macbeth imagined she heard an owl scream and the crickets cry. Suddenly, Macbeth returned.

Lady Macbeth: Who's there? My husband!

Macbeth is upset by his actions. He should be shown to be very nervous.

Macbeth: I have done the deed, but methought I heard a voice cry, "Sleep no more! Macbeth does murder sleep! Macbeth shall sleep no more!" Look at my hands! They are bloody!

Lady Macbeth: Wash this filthy witness from your hands. But why did you bring these daggers from the place? Go back and smear Duncan's sleeping guards with blood.

Macbeth: I'll go no more; I am afraid to think what I have done. Look on it again, I dare not.

Lady Macbeth: Give me the daggers! I'll do it! (Leaves.)

Page Ten

Macbeth: (Knocking is heard.) Whence is that knocking? How is it with me when every noise appalls me?

Lady Macbeth: (Returns.) My hands are bloody now, too, but I am not a coward. A little water clears us of this deed. I hear knocking. Hark, more knocking! Get on your nightgown, and be ready to greet whoever has come to our gate.

As Macbeth and his wife change, a porter opened the front gate to admit Macduff and Lennox, two of King Duncan's men. They are greeted by Macbeth.

Macbeth: Good morrow, both.

Macduff: Is the king stirring?

Macbeth: Not yet.

Macduff: I'll make so bold as to wake him. (Exits, and cries aloud from behind the backgrounds.) O horror! Horror! (Re-enters.)

Page Eleven

The Comedy of Errors

(Holiday Adaptation)

Performance Length	Number of Parts	Genre
10 to 15 Minutes	14	Comedy

Synopsis

This is a play of mistaken identities. Syracuse and Ephesus are at war, and it is death to any who enters their enemy's city. Egeon, a merchant of Syracuse looking for his missing wife, his twin sons, and their twin attendants, enters Ephesus and is captured, and sentenced to death. However, his sad tale of a family divided by a shipwreck, buys him some time to raise the funds necessary to pay his way out of the death sentence. Unknown to him, his wife, one son, and one attendant, separated from him during the shipwreck, have been living in Ephesus all these years. And to confuse matters, the son and attendant who have lived with him since the shipwreck have also entered Ephesus, looking for their lost family members. Needless to say, there are several comic scenes of mistaken identities, that all end well with the entire family being reunited.

Characters

Reading Levels of Difficulty:

Non-Speaking (NS)   **Easy (E)**   **Moderate (M)**   **Challenging (C)**

Duke Solinus **(M)**   Antipholus of Syracuse **(C)**   Egeon **(C)**
Dromio of Syracuse **(C)**   Emilia, Egeon's wife/Abbess of a Priory **(E)**
Antipholus of Ephesus **(M)**   Dromio of Ephesus **(C)**   Adriana **(E)**
Luciana **(E)**   Merchant **(M)**   Jailor **(NS)**
Officer 1 **(NS)**   Officer 2 **(NS)**   Narrator **(M)**

Pronunciation Guide

Antipholus (an-tiff-uh-lus)   **Egeon** (ee'-gee-un)

Staging & Costumes

The staging can be accomplished very simply. Props are not required. Weapons are mimed. Costumes are similar to other play suggestions, except for the Antipholus twins and the Dromio twins. For help with these characters, please see the costume ideas in the "Suggestions for Performing the Plays" section (page 8) in the Teacher Guide at the front of the book.

Teaching Tips

- What makes us laugh? Brainstorm ideas. What is funny about this play?
- Why is this play called *The Comedy of Errors*? Brainstorm ideas.
- Brainstorm a list of books, plays, movies, etc., in which twins appear, and, perhaps, find themselves in mix-ups.

Extension Activities

- What other trouble could identical twins get into? Write a story.
- How else could you perform this play so that the twins could be easily identified, and yet confused as well?
- Draw a picture of your favorite scene in the play/write a paragraph telling why you chose it.

The Comedy of Errors
(Holiday Adaptation)

Dramatis Personae

Duke Solinus –

Antipholus of Syracuse –

Egeon –

Dromio of Syracuse –

Emilia, Egeon's wife, &
an Abbess of a Priory –

Antipholus of Ephesus –

Dromio of Ephesus –

Adriana –

Luciana –

Merchant –

Jailor –

Officer 1 –

Officer 2 –

Narrator –

Adriana: I see two husbands, and two attendants!

Antipholus of S.: And I see Egeon, my father!

Abbess: Egeon? Hadst thou a wife once called Emilia that bore you two fair sons? If thou be Egeon, speak! And speak unto the same Emilia!

Speech bubble: There is true joy here because the family is reunited after many years. Let your voices show their joy.

Egeon: If I dream not, thou art my lost wife, Emilia!

Duke Solinus: Old man of Syracuse, the story that you told of a wife, of twin sons, of twin servants, and a shipwreck at sea, has proven true! I set you free!

In the end, all debts were paid, Adriana laughed at the story with her husband, and Egeon's family was finally reunited after all these long years of grief. Happily, the two Dromio's were also reunited, and together with the Duke and Egeon's entire family, went to Emilia's priory for great feasting and celebrating.

It is a time of conflict in ancient Greece. The two great cities, Ephesus and Syracuse, have long been at war, and if any citizen should enter the enemy's city, the penalty is death! It is into this scene that Egeon, an aged merchant from Syracuse, wanders and is arrested, while in search of his lost family.

Duke Solinus: Merchant of Syracuse, plead no more. For being in Ephesus, thou art condemned to die.

Egeon: My woes will end like the evening sun.

Duke Solinus: Well, Syracusian, say in brief for what cause thou cam'st to Ephesus.

Egeon: I speak of griefs unspeakable. I am a merchant, born in Syracuse, with a wife who was the joyful mother of our two goodly sons, twin boys, the one so like the other as could not be distinguished but by names. I also took twin boys into my house to attend my sons. Once, while away from home, our ship was wrecked by the always-wind-obeying deep, and my wife, one of my goodly sons, and one of our attendants were swept away.

Page Two

Adriana: I come for my husband. He has gone mad!

Abbess: No, he took this place for sanctuary.
(Exit Abbess.)

Eventually, the whole problem was sorted out as Egeon was being led to his execution by Duke Solinus. Egeon had been unable to raise the money to save his life.

Duke Solinus: What is this?

Adriana: Justice, most sacred duke, against the Abbess. My husband, Antipholus, has gone mad and is inside.

(Enter Antipholus and Dromio of Ephesus with Officer 1.)

Antipholus of E.: Grant me justice, most gracious duke!

Egeon: My son, Antipholus, and Dromio!

Antipholus of E.: I never saw you in my life till now!

Egeon: Tell me thou art my son, Antipholus!

Antipholus of E.: I never saw my father in all my life.

(Enter the Abbess with Antipholus and Dromio of Syracuse.)

Abbess: Most mighty duke, behold a man much wronged.

Page Eleven

Duke Solinus: Go on, for we may pity, though not pardon thee.

Egeon: Many years later, my other son, Antipholus, became inquisitive after his brother, and with his attendant, Dromio, left on a quest to find them. Now they too are lost, and I have spent five years wandering Greece looking for them, ending here in Ephesus.

Duke Solinus: Hapless Egeon, whom the fates have marked to bear the extremity of dire mishap. Were it not against our laws, I would pardon thee, but I cannot. However, I will favor thee in what I can. I give you one day to try all thy friends thou hast in Ephesus; beg thou, borrow, to make up the sum of one thousand marks to quit the penalty and live. If no, then thou are doomed to die. Jailor, take him to thy custody.

What Egeon didn't know was that when his wife, his son, and their attendant were lost in the shipwreck, they came to live in Ephesus, thinking the others were drowned. This son was also called Antipholus, and his attendant was also called Dromio. And to confuse matters further, the son and his attendant, who set out to find the rest of his family, were at

Page Three

Dromio of E.: O villain! Thou hast stolen both mine office and my name!

Antipholus of E.: Go, fetch me something, I'll break open the gate!

Luckily, Antipholus of Ephesus did not break down his door, but instead went away with Dromio to calm himself. Later, they faced even more problems when they were arrested over unpaid money, having been confused with Antipholus and Dromio of Syracuse! Even Adriana, his wife, did not believe him, and thought he had gone mad.

After Antipholus and Dromio of Ephesus were taken away by an officer, Antipholus and Dromio of Syracuse, having just faced their own strange problems, came around the corner, with swords drawn.

Luciana: They are loose again, mistress!

Adriana: And come with naked swords! Call for more help!

[Enter Officer 2.]

Dromio of S.: Master! This is a priory here. Run inside, and seek sanctuary, or we are spoiled. *[Exit, into the priory.]*

[Enter Abbess.]

Abbess: What is this noise?

Page Ten

that moment also in Ephesus. Needless to say, with two pairs of identical twins in the same city, confusion and mistaken identities became the order of the day!

Once in Ephesus, Antipholus of Syracuse met a merchant, his old friend.

Merchant: Say you are from Epidamnum, because, Antipholus, this very day a Syracusian merchant was apprehended for arrival here, and dies ere the weary sun is set. Be careful! There is your money I kept.

Antipholus of S.: Dromio, take my money to the Centaur Inn, where we are staying, and remain there till I come.

Dromio of S.: I will, my lord. *(Exit Dromio of S.)*

Antipholus of S.: Will you walk with me, my friend, and dine with me at my inn?

Merchant: I crave your pardon, but I cannot. I'll meet with you at mart. My present business calls me from you.

Antipholus of S.: Farewell till then.
(Enter Dromio of Ephesus.)
Here comes Dromio. What now? Returned so soon?

Page Four

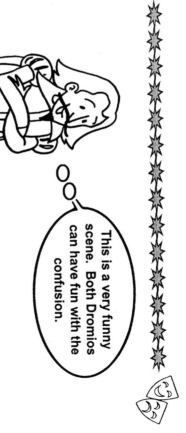

This is a very funny scene. Both Dromios can have fun with the confusion.

Antipholus of E.: I think thou art a donkey! But here is my house, and the door is locked!

Dromio of E.: Maud, Bridget, Marian, Cicely, Gillian, Gin! Open the door.

Dromio of S.: *(From within the house.)* Get thee from the door!

Dromio of E.: My master stays in the street! Open!

Dromio of S.: *(From within.)* Let him walk from whence he came!

Antipholus of E.: Who talks within? Ho! Open the door!

Dromio of S.: *(From within.)* Not today! Come again when you may!

Antipholus of E.: What art thou, that keep'st me from my own house?

Dromio of S.: *(From within.)* The porter, for this time, and my name is Dromio.

Page Nine

The sequence of mistaken identities begins here. Even Antipholus of Syracuse cannot tell that this is a different Dromio! Dromio must be **very** surprised and confused.

Dromio of E.: Returned so soon? Rather approached too late.

Antipholus of S.: Where have you left the money I gave you?

Dromio of E.: The sixpence I had o' Wednesday? I kept it not.

Antipholus of S.: I am not in a sportive humor now. Where is the gold I gave thee?

Dromio of E.: To me, sir? Why you gave no gold to me. I come from my mistress in haste, to bring thee home.

Antipholus of S.: Come, Dromio, these jests are out of season. I have no wife nor home here.

Dromio of E.: I do not know of what you speak.

Page Five

Antipholus of S.: Villain, thou liest! For even her very words didst thou deliver to me on the mart.

Dromio of S.: I never spake with her in all my life.

Antipholus of S.: How can she thus, then call us by our names?

Dromio of S.: I know not!

Luciana: Dromio, go bid the servants spread for dinner.

Dromio of S.: This is the fairy land! I am transformed, master am I not.

Antipholus of S.: I think thou art in mind, and so am I.

Adriana: Come, let us go to dinner.

Later, as Antipholus of Ephesus walked home for dinner, he saw Dromio of Ephesus coming toward them.

Antipholus of E.: Here comes the villain that said that I beat him in the mart, and that I did deny my wife and house! Thou drunkard, why didst thou mean by this?

Dromio of E.: Say what you will sir, but I know what I know. That you chased and beat me at the mart.

Page Eight

66

Antipholus of S.: I'll teach you to cheat me! *(Dromio runs away.)*

Later, and still angry, Antipholus of Syracuse met Dromio of Syracuse and confronted him.

Antipholus of S.: How now, sir? Is your merry humor altered? Why did you answer me so madly?

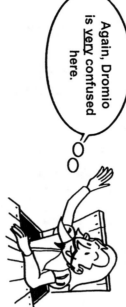

Again, Dromio is **very** confused here.

Dromio of S.: What answer sir? When spake I such a word? I haven't seen you since you sent me hence.

Antipholus of S.: Villain, thou didst deny the gold's receipt.

Dromio of S.: What means this jest? I pray you master, tell me.

Antipholus of S.: Thinkest thou I jest? Take that!
(He "hits" Dromio. NOTE: Mime this only! Do not hit the other student!)

Into this scene, came Adriana, the wife of Antipholus of Ephesus, and her sister, Luciana.

Antipholus of S.: Who waves us yonder?

Adriana: Ay, ay, Antipholus, why look strange and frown?
(Tries to hug him, but he pulls back.)
Ah, do not tear thyself from me.

Antipholus of S.: Plead you to me, fair dame? I know you not. In Ephesus, I am but two hours.

Luciana: Fie, brother! My sister sent for you by Dromio.

Antipholus of S.: By Dromio?

Dromio of S.: By me?

Adriana: And when he returned to me, he said that you chased and beat him.

Antipholus of S.: Dromio, didst thou converse, sir, with this gentlewoman?

Dromio of S.: I sir? I never saw her till this time.

 OTM-1867 • SSR1-67 Shakespeare Shorts

A Midsummer Night's Dream

(Holiday Adaptation)

Performance Length	Number of Parts	Genre
15 to 20 Minutes	23	Comedy

Synopsis

Long ago, in Athens, three groups of people come together one midsummer's evening in an enchanted wood. One group, Hermia, Lysander, Helena, and Demetrius, are sorting out lovers' issues. A second group, a group of actors, is preparing a play for the Duke's wedding. The final group is made up of the fairies who live in the woods. Many tricks are played, all resulting in the wrong people loving each other, but in the end, everyone ends up with the correct person.

Characters

Reading Levels of Difficulty:
Non-Speaking (NS)　　**Easy (E)**　　**Moderate (M)**　　**Challenging (C)**

Duke Theseus **(C)**	Hippolyta, his fiancé **(E)**	Hermia **(M)**	Lysander **(M)**
Helena **(M)**	Demetrius **(M)**	Peter Quince **(C)**	Nick Bottom **(C)**
Francis Flute **(M)**	Tom Snout **(E)**	Robin Starveling **(E)**	Snug **(E)**
Egeus **(M)**	Oberon, the Fairy King **(C)**	Titania, the Fairy Queen **(M)**	
Puck, or Robin Goodfellow **(C)**		Fairy **(M)**	Peasblossom **(E)**
Cobweb **(E)**	Mustardseed **(E)**	Moth **(E)**	Philostrate **(E)**
Narrator **(M)**			

Pronunciation Guide

Many of the names in this play are from ancient Greece.
Theseus (thee'-see-us)　　　　　　　　　**Helena** (hel'-e-na or hel-ay'-na)
Demetrius (de-mee'-tree-us)

Staging & Costumes

Decorating the stage with some kind of artificial tree or shrub, hung with small Christmas tree lights, is an effective way of lending a dreamlike aura to the stage; it looks as if small, twinkling fairies have appeared in the trees. Titania will need something to sleep on, perhaps some gym mats, stacked four or five high, covered by a floral shower curtain or other fabric.

To make the fairies special, you might want to make fairy wings out of cardboard, covered with aluminum foil or a lacy cloth. Puck is effective if he is dressed in green, as a spirit of the woods might be. The highlight is, of course, Nick Bottom and his donkey head. Try attaching the donkey head suggested in the Teacher Guide (page 9) to a baseball cap; it's easy to put on and remove as needed.

Teaching Tips

- Emphasize the dreamlike quality of this play, much of which happens at night.
- The fairies should speak as a chorus, with a musical lilt in their voices.
- Bottom and Puck should be fairly strong, because they must speak clearly and carry several scenes.
- Have Nick Bottom and Francis Flute really overact during the play at the end for comic effect.

Extension Activities

- Compare the fairies in this story with those in other stories (How are they similar? Different?)
- What was ancient Athens like? What were its laws? What were its customs? Look at buildings, art, and pictures, etc., to give some background.

A Midsummer Night's Dream
(Holiday Adaptation)

Dramatis Personae

Duke Theseus –
Hippolyta, his fiancé –
Hermia –
Lysander –
Helena –
Demetrius –
Peter Quince –
Nick Bottom –
Francis Flute –
Tom Snout –
Snug –
Robin Starveling –
Egeus –
Oberon, the Fairy King –
Titania, the Fairy Queen –
Puck, or Robin Goodfellow –
Fairy –
Peasblossom –
Cobweb –
Moth –
Mustardseed –
Philostrate –
Narrator –

Page One

Flute: *(Looking at Bottom.)*
Asleep, my love? What dead, my dove?
Quite dumb?
Thus Thisbe ends too, adieu, adieu, adieu.
(He falls.)

(Silence, followed by light clapping.)

Bottom: *(Jumping up.)*
Will it please you to hear an epilogue, or to see
a dance between two of our company?

Theseus: No! Please!

(Everyone laughs. As they leave the stage, enter Puck alone.)

Puck: If we shadows have offended,
Think but this, and all is mended,
That you have slumbered here
While these visions did appear.
Give me your hands, if we be friends,
And we shall all restore amends.

Page Sixteen

Long ago, in Athens, Duke Theseus and his fiancé, Hippolyta, busied themselves with preparations for their upcoming wedding. In the middle of their discussions, a man named Egeus entered the palace with his daughter Hermia, and two men named Lysander and Demetrius.

Duke Theseus: Now, fair Hippolyta, our nuptial hour draws on apace.

Hippolyta: In four happy days, the moon, like to a silver bow new bent in Heaven, shall behold the night of our solemnities.

Duke Theseus: Go, Philostrate, awake the pert and nimble spirit of mirth in Athens!

(Exit Philostrate. Enter Egeus, Hermia, Lysander, and Demetrius.)

Duke Theseus: Thanks, good Egeus. What's the news with thee?

Egeus: Happy be Theseus, our renowned duke!

Duke Theseus: Thanks, good Egeus. What's the news with thee?

Egeus: Full of vexation come I, with complaint against my daughter Hermia. Stand forth, Demetrius: this man hath my consent to marry Hermia. Stand forth, Lysander: this man hath bewitched her heart. As she is mine, I beg the ancient

Page Two

So Bottom woke up changed back into a man, and he ran to tell his friends.

Everything ended happily. The duke was married, Hermia's father, Egeus, realizing his daughter's true love, allowed Hermia to married Lysander, and Demetrius married Helena, and they all lived happily ever after.

At the duke's wedding, the actors performed the play before the duke, his new wife, and all the others.

Philostrate: So please you grace, they are ready.

Theseus: Then let them begin.

(Have Bottom and the others mime a short scene, as the narrator reads.)

After awhile, everyone realized that the play was not really very good.

Hippolyta: This is the silliest stuff I ever heard!

Bottom and Flute must really overact here.

Bottom: Now I am dead! Now I am fled! Now die, die, die, die, die! *(He falls.)*

Page Fifteen

privilege of Athens: as she is mine, so I choose her husband, or to her death, according to our law.

Duke Theseus: What say you, Hermia? Demetrius is a worthy gentleman.

Hermia: So is Lysander. I would my father looked but with my eyes.

Duke Theseus: Rather, your eyes must with his judgment look. Take time to think, and by the next new moon, upon that day either prepare to die for disobedience to your father's will, or else, to wed Demetrius, as he would.

(Exit all but Hermia and Lysander.)

Hermia was very scared, but she and Lysander made a secret plan.

Lysander: Hear me, Hermia. I have an aunt, whose house is remote from Athens. We'll sneak away to my aunt's house, and there, gentle Hermia, may I marry there. To that place, the sharp Athenian law cannot pursue us.

Page Three

- -

While Oberon laughed at his wife, he noticed that Puck had sprinkled the flower juice into the wrong man's eyes. He called Puck to him, and told him to fix the problem. So Puck put all four of them, Hermia, Lysander, Demetrius, and Helena, to sleep, and when they woke up, everything was fine: Lysander loved Hermia, and now Demetrius loved Helena.

Oberon decided that he was finished tricking his wife, so he went to her and found her sleeping. He removed the spell from her.

Oberon: Now, my Titania, wake you, my sweet queen.

Titania: Oh, what a dream I had. I dreamed I was in love with a donkey!

Oberon: Their lies your love. *(Points to Nick Bottom.)*

Titania: How came these things to pass?

Oberon: *(Gently.)* Silence now, and do not worry. I am no longer angry with you. Robin, come here! Take off this donkey's head.

Puck: I will do this, my lord, but hurry, for I do hear the morning lark.

Page Fourteen

Hermia: My good Lysander! I swear to thee by Cupid's strongest bow, tomorrow truly will I meet with thee.

Lysander: Keep promise, love. Look, here comes Helena.

(Enter Helena.)

Hermia: God speed, fair Helena.

Helena: Demetrius loves you fair. Were the world mine, I would teach him to love me.

Hermia: I frown upon him.

Lysander: Helena, to you our minds we will unfold. Tomorrow night, we leave Athens to marry at my aunt's house in the woods.

Helena: How happy some can be!

Hermia and Lysander: Good night, Helena! (They both exit.)

Page Four

Titania: Thou art as wise as thou art beautiful. Come here my fairies.

(Enter Peasblossom, Cobweb, Moth, and Mustardseed.)

The fairies should speak in an almost musical manner when speaking in unison.

Fairies: We are here!

Titania: Be kind and courteous to this gentleman. Feed him with dewberries. And when night falls, fan the moonbeams from his sleeping eyes.

Fairies: We will!

Bottom: What are your names? I wish to know you better.

(Each calls out her name as they leave, following Titania, and gently surrounding and pulling Bottom offstage.)

Fairies: Peasblossom! Cobweb! Moth! Mustardseed!

Page Thirteen

Helena: I must go and tell Demetrius, and perhaps then he will love me!

(speech bubble) Helena isn't thinking clearly here, because by trying to win Demetrius' love, she is betraying her friends' confidence.

That same day, in another part of Athens, some men were getting ready to perform a play at the Duke's wedding. Peter Quince was in charge. One of the other men was named Nick Bottom. His part in the play was to be a handsome hero.

Peter Quince: Is all our company here? Answer as I call you. Nick Bottom, the weaver?

Bottom: Ready. Which part do I have?

(speech bubble) Always portray Nick Bottom as pompous and full of himself. Peter Quince must be shown as someone in charge.

Page Five

(Re-enter Bottom with a donkey's head.)

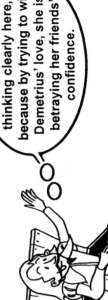

Bottom: As true as truest horse, that yet would never tire.

(speech bubble) The other actors are truly frightened by Bottom's transformation.

Peter Quince: Help! We are haunted! Fly masters!

Bottom: Why do they run away? What do you see?

Snout: O, Bottom, thou art changed!

Starveling: What do I see on thee?

Flute: Bless thee, Bottom, thou art translated!

(Exit Quince, Starveling, Snout, Snug, and Flute. Titania awakes and sees Bottom.)

Titania: What angel wakes me from my flowery bed? Thou art beautiful. Mine eye is enthralled to thy shape. I swear I love thee.

Bottom: Methinks, mistress, you should have little reason for that. And yet, reason and love keep little company now-a-days.

Page Twelve

Page Six

Peter Quince: You are set down for Pyramus.

Bottom: What is Pyramus? A lover or a tyrant?

Peter Quince: A lover that kills himself most gallant for love.

Bottom: Oh, I will be wonderful! I will move storms. The ladies will all love me!

Peter Quince: Francis Flute, the bellows-mender?

Flute: Here, Peter Quince.

Peter Quince: Flute, you must take Thisbe on you.

Flute: What is Thisbe? A wandering knight?

Peter Quince: It is the lady that Pyramus must love.

Flute: Nay, let me not play a woman! I have a beard coming!

Peter Quince: Robin Starveling, the tailor? *(Starveling raises his hand.)* You must play Thisbe's mother. Tom Snout, the tinker? *(Snout raises his hand.)* You are Pyramus' father. Snug, the joiner? *(Snug raises his hand.)* You are the lion, and do nothing but roaring.

Page Six

Page Eleven

Puck: What hempen homespuns have we swaggering here? So near the cradle of the fairy queen! I'll listen.

Peter Quince: Speak Pyramus; Thisbe come forth.

Bottom: Thisbe, the flowers of odious savors sweet.

Peter Quince: No! Odors, odors sweet!

Bottom: — odors savors sweet.

Flute: Must I speak now?

Peter Quince: Ay, marry, you must.

Flute: *(Poorly imitating a woman's voice.)* I'll meet thee, Pyramus, at Ninny's tomb.

Quince: No! Ninus' tomb. Now, Pyramus, exit for a moment. *(Exit Bottom.)* Wait, Pyramus; now enter, your cue is past.

Peter Quince gets frustrated by Bottom and Flute's errors!

Page Eleven

Bottom: Let me play the lion too! I shall roar...

Peter Quince: ...and fright the ladies out of their wits, and get us all hanged. That's enough, Nick Bottom. We'll all meet tomorrow night in the woods, by the duke's oak tree to practice our play. Don't forget!

Now in these same woods lived the fairies. Oberon was their king, and Titania was their queen.

Puck is a playful character, who enjoys playing tricks on others.

Puck: How now, spirit! Whither wander you?

Fairy: Over hill, over dale, I do wander everywhere, And I serve the fairy queen. I must go and seek dewdrops here, because our queen and her elves come here anon.

Puck: The king doth keep his revels here tonight, and he is full of wrath at the queen, and jealous.

Fairy: You are that shrewd and knavish sprite called Robin Goodfellow, that plays tricks on people. Some call you sweet Puck. Are you not he?

Page Seven

Oberon felt sorry for Helena, so when Puck returned with the flower, he told him to sprinkle it in Demetrius' eyes too.

(Enter Puck.)

Oberon: I know a bank with sweet roses where Titania sleeps, sometimes of the night. With this juice I'll streak here eyes. And take thou some and find in these woods a sweet Athenian lady who is in love with a disdainful youth. Anoint his eyes, but only when the first thing he sees may be the lady.

Puck: Fear not, my lord! Your servant shall do so.

As Puck left, Hermia and Lysander entered the woods. Oberon soon found Titania asleep by a brook, and he sprinkled the flower juice on her eyes. But, as Puck looked for Helena and Demetrius, he found Hermia and Lysander instead, and he made them fall asleep. He thought these were the people Oberon had been talking about, so he sprinkled the flower juice on Lysander's eyes. *(Enter Helena.)* When Lysander woke up, he saw Helena looking for Demetrius, and he fell in love with her. He chased her into the woods leaving Hermia behind.

Puck also found Nick Bottom and the other actors in the woods rehearsing near where Titania slept. He decided to play a trick on them by giving Bottom a donkey's head.

Page Ten

Puck: Thou speakest aright. I am that merry wanderer of the night. I jest to Oberon, and make him smile. But room, fairy, here comes Oberon.

Fairy: And here comes my mistress too.

(Enter Oberon, on one side, and Titania, with four fairies, on the other.)

Oberon: Ill met by moonlight, Titania.

Titania: What, jealous Oberon? Come fairies, away, let's skip by.

(Exit Titania and fairies.)

Unfortunately, Oberon and Titania had had an argument, and were angry with each other. Since fairies liked to play tricks on people, Oberon decided to play a trick on his queen. He called Puck to help him.

Oberon: My gentle Puck, come hither. Fetch me that flower, the juice of it on sleeping eyelids laid, that makes a man or woman love the first living creature that it sees.

Puck: I'll find it for you, King Oberon, even if I have to fly round about the Earth. *(Exit.)*

Page Eight

Oberon: Having this flower, I'll watch Titania when she is asleep, and sprinkle its juice on her sleeping eyes. She'll fall in love with whatever first she sees, be it a lion, a bull, or a meddling monkey! That will teach her! *(Pauses, listening.)* But who comes here? I am invisible, and will overhear their conference.

As Oberon listened, Demetrius and Helena entered the woods, looking for Hermia and Lysander.

Demetrius: I love thee not; therefore pursue me not. Where are Lysander and Hermia? Get thee gone, and follow me no more. I cannot love you.

Helena: And for that do I love you the more.

Demetrius: But I am sick when I do look on thee.

Helena: And I am sick when I do not look on you!

Oberon: Fare thee well, nymph, ere he do leave this grove, thou shalt fly him, and he shall seek thy love.

(Exit Demetrius and Helena.)

Page Nine

Name: _____

Shakespeare Comprehension Check

Play Title: _____

Which kind of play is this? (Circle one.)

tragedy   comedy   history   problem play/romance

Explain how you know. _____
_____
_____

Who is the main character in your play? _____

Describe your main character by completing the chart.

Personality Trait	Which actions show this in the play?	What is the result of these actions?

What is the main character's motivation for acting in these ways?
_____
_____
_____

Where and **when** does your play take place? Tell about the setting, focusing on time and place.
_____
_____
_____

What is the problem in your play? **How** is it resolved?
_____
_____
_____

Shakespeare Writing Project

This project is designed to let you write about Shakespeare in many different ways. Some parts will be true, and some will require your imagination to think of what it was like to live in Shakespeare's day.

For this assignment, you must complete something from each of the sections below. Everyone must complete all of Part A, and then complete two activities from Part B. You may work on these activities in any order you wish.

Part A: Nonfiction

- **My Thoughts on William Shakespeare**
  Use the plan on the next page to write about Shakespeare's life and your experiences with his plays. You may wish to add extra details by completing extra research in the library.

- **My Character in Shakespeare**
  Who are you? Which play is yours? What is your character like? Decide how best to present this information (examples: as a diary entry, as a newspaper story, or, perhaps, as a piece of nonfiction writing).

Part B: Fiction

- **My Day with William Shakespeare**
  Pretend you went to London, met William Shakespeare, and spent the day with him in the Globe Theatre preparing for your play. What would he be like? What would he show you? What would you do? Be imaginative!

- **The Day I Acted in the Globe Theatre**
  Pretend you went to London and acted in a play by Shakespeare, in Shakespeare's time, at the Globe Theatre. Which play would it be? How would Shakespeare help you? How would the audience react to your acting? Be imaginative!

- **My Interview with William Shakespeare**
  Your local newspaper, TV station, or radio station has given you the assignment of going back in time to interview William Shakespeare. Where would the interview take place? What questions would you ask him? How would he respond? Be imaginative!

- **My Short Shakespearean Play**
  Write a brief play in the style of William Shakespeare. What would the time period be for your setting (examples: past, present, or future)? Would some familiar characters appear in your play? How would a modern day event be presented in authentic Shakespearean language? Perhaps retell a favorite story as a play by Shakespeare. Be creative!

My Thoughts on William Shakespeare

Write a six- to eight-paragraph life story of William Shakespeare using what you have learned about him in class. You may use your *All about William Shakespeare* biography page as a guide, as well as including anything else you may have learned in your independent research. Please write in your own words.

Here is a guide to help you. You may follow this plan if you wish.

Paragraph 1: Who was Shakespeare? Why do we remember him? What makes him special?

Paragraph 2: Where was he born? Where did he grow up? What do we know about his childhood and education?

Paragraph 3: Who was in his family? Who did he marry? Did they have any children?

Paragraph 4: Where did Shakespeare go to write his plays? In which famous building did he work? Name some of his plays. What was the theater like in Shakespeare's day? Compare it with today (examples: movies, live theater, etc.).

Paragraph 5: Describe The Globe Theatre. What was it like? What was the audience like? How much did it cost to attend? Were the theaters ever closed for unusual reasons? What happened in The Globe Theatre that made Shakespeare decide to retire from the theater?

Paragraph 6: Choose your favorite play and write about it. What is it about? Why do you like it? Why do you think we still like to watch it today?

Paragraph 7: Compare Shakespeare to one of your favorite authors of today. How are they similar? How are they different? Give your opinions on each.

Paragraph 8: What have you enjoyed most about learning about Shakespeare? What was your favorite thing? Give your thoughts about rehearsing and performing Shakespeare as well. What was difficult? What was most satisfying? Explain your thoughts.

Name: _____

Shakespeare Festival

Follow-Up Activity

My favorite part of our Shakespeare Festival was _____

_____

_____

_____

_____

My favorite play was: (Circle one.)

Henry IV	Richard II	The Comedy of Errors	Romeo and Juliet
Julius Caesar	Richard III	A Midsummer Night's Dream	Macbeth

I liked it best because _____

_____

_____

_____

Here are my feelings about:

• rehearsing for a play and learning my lines:

_____

_____

_____

_____

• acting on the stage:

_____

_____

_____

_____

• my performance in my play:

_____

_____

_____

_____

Publication Listing

See Dealer or www.sslearning.com For Pricing 1-800-463-6367

Code #	Title and Grade
SSC1-12	A Time of Plenty Gr. 2
SSN1-92	Abel's Island NS 4-6
SSF1-16	Aboriginal Peoples of Canada Gr. 7-8
SSK1-31	Addition & Subtraction Drills Gr. 1-3
SSK1-28	Addition Drills Gr. 1-3
SSY1-04	Addition Gr. 1-3
SSN1-174	Adv. of Huckle Berry Finn NS 7-8
SSB1-63	African Animals Gr 4-6
SSB1-29	All About Bears Gr. 1-2
SSF1-08	All About Boats Gr. 2-3
SSJ1-02	All About Canada Gr. 2
SSB1-54	All About Cattle Gr. 4-6
SSN1-10	All About Colours Gr. P-1
SSB1-93	All About Dinosaurs Gr. 2
SSN1-14	All About Dragons Gr. 3-5
SSB1-07	All About Elephants Gr. 3-4
SSB1-68	All About Fish Gr. 4-6
SSN1-39	All About Giants Gr. 2-3
SSH1-15	All About Jobs Gr. 1-3
SSH1-05	All About Me Gr. 1
SSA1-02	All About Mexico Gr. 4-6
SSR1-28	All About Nouns Gr. 5-7
SSF1-09	All About Planes Gr. 2-3
SSB1-33	All About Plants Gr. 2-3
SSR1-29	All About Pronouns Gr. 5-7
SSB1-12	All About Rabbits Gr. 2-3
SSB1-58	All About Spiders Gr. 4-6
SSA1-03	All About the Desert Gr. 4-6
SSA1-04	All About the Ocean Gr. 5-7
SSZ1-01	All About the Olympics Gr. 2-4
SSB1-49	All About the Sea Gr. 4-6
SSK1-06	All About Time Gr. 4-6
SSF1-07	All About Trains Gr. 2-3
SSH1-18	All About Transportation Gr. 2
SSB1-01	All About Trees Gr. 4-6
SSB1-61	All About Weather Gr. 7-8
SSB1-06	All About Whales Gr. 3-4
SSPC-26	All Kinds of Clocks B/W Pictures
SSB1-110	All Kinds of Structures Gr. 1
SSH1-19	All Kinds of Vehicles Gr. 3
SSF1-01	Amazing Aztecs Gr. 4-6
SSB1-92	Amazing Earthworms Gr. 2-3
SSJ1-50	Amazing Facts in Canadian History Gr. 4-6
SSB1-32	Amazing Insects Gr. 4-6
SSN1-132	Amelia Bedelia–Camping NS 1-3
SSN1-68	Amelia Bedelia NS 1-3
SSN1-155	Amelia Bedelia-Surprise Shower NS 1-3
SSA1-13	America The Beautiful Gr. 4-6
SSN1-57	Amish Adventure NS 7-8
SSF1-02	Ancient China Gr. 4-6
SSF1-18	Ancient Egypt Gr. 4-6
SSF1-21	Ancient Greece Gr. 4-6
SSF1-19	Ancient Rome Gr. 4-6
SSQ1-06	Animal Town – Big Book Pkg 1-3
SSQ1-02	Animals Prepare Winter – Big Book Pkg 1-3
SSN1-150	Animorphs the Invasion NS 4-6
SSN1-53	Anne of Green Gables NS 7-8
SSB1-40	Apple Celebration Gr. 4-6
SSB1-04	Apple Mania Gr. 2-3
SSB1-38	Apples are the Greatest Gr. P-K
SSB1-59	Arctic Animals Gr. 4-6
SSN1-162	Arnold Lobel Author Study Gr. 2-3
SSPC-22	Australia B/W Pictures
SSA1-05	Australia Gr. 5-8
SSM1-03	Autumn in the Woodlot Gr. 2-3
SSM1-08	Autumn Wonders Gr. 1
SSN1-41	Baby Sister for Frances NS 1-3
SSPC-19	Back to School B/W Pictures
SSC1-33	Back to School Gr. 2-3
SSN1-224	Banner in the Sky NS 7-8
SSN1-36	Bargain for Frances NS 1-3
SSB1-82	Bats Gr. 4-6
SSN1-71	BB – Drug Free Zone NS Gr. 1-3
SSN1-88	BB – In the Freaky House NS 1-3
SSN1-78	BB – Media Madness NS 1-3
SSN1-69	BB – Wheelchair Commando NS 1-3
SSN1-119	Be a Perfect Person-3 Days NS 4-6

Code #	Title and Grade
SSC1-15	Be My Valentine Gr. 1
SSD1-01	Be Safe Not Sorry Gr. P-1
SSN1-09	Bear Tales Gr. 2-4
SSB1-28	Bears Gr. 4-6
SSN1-202	Bears in Literature Gr. 1-3
SSN1-40	Beatrix Potter Gr. 2-4
SSN1-129	Beatrix Potter: Activity Biography 2-4
SSB1-47	Beautiful Bugs Gr. 1
SSB1-21	Beavers Gr. 3-5
SSN1-257	Because of Winn-Dixie NS Gr. 4-6
SSN1-33	Bedtime for Frances NS 1-3
SSN1-114	Best Christmas Pageant Ever NS 4-6
SSN1-32	Best Friends for Frances NS 1-3
SSB1-39	Best Friends Pets Gr. P-K
SSN1-185	BFG NS Gr. 4-6
SSN1-35	Birthday for Frances NS Gr. 1-3
SSN1-107	Borrowers NS Gr. 4-6
SSC1-16	Bouquet of Valentines Gr. 2
SSN1-29	Bread & Jam for Frances NS 1-3
SSN1-63	Bridge to Terabithia NS Gr. 4-6
SSY1-24	BTS Numeración Gr. 1-3
SSY1-25	BTS Adición Gr. 1-3
SSY1-26	BTS Sustracción Gr. 1-3
SSY1-27	BTS Fonética Gr. 1-3
SSY1-28	BTS Leer para Entender Gr. 1-3
SSY1-29	BTS Uso de las Mayúsculas y Reglas de Puntuación Gr. 1-3
SSY1-30	BTS Composición de Oraciones Gr. 1-3
SSY1-31	BTS Composici13n de Historias Gr. 1-3
SSN1-256	Bud, Not Buddy NS Gr. 4-6
SSB1-31	Bugs, Bugs & More Bugs Gr. 2-3
SSR1-07	Building Word Families L.V. 1-2
SSR1-05	Building Word Families S.V. 1-2
SSN1-204	Bunnicula NS Gr. 4-6
SSB1-80	Butterflies & Caterpillars Gr. 1-2
SSN1-164	Call It Courage NS Gr. 7-8
SSN1-67	Call of the Wild NS Gr. 7-8
SSJ1-41	Canada & It's Trading Partners 6-8
SSPC-28	Canada B/W Pictures
SSN1-173	Canada Geese Quilt NS Gr. 4-6
SSJ1-01	Canada Gr. 1
SSJ1-33	Canada's Capital Cities Gr. 4-6
SSJ1-43	Canada's Confederation Gr. 7-8
SSF1-04	Canada's First Nations Gr. 7-8
SSJ1-51	Canada's Landmarks Gr. 1-3
SSJ1-48	Canada's Landmarks Gr. 4-6
SSJ1-42	Canada's Traditions & Celeb. Gr. 1-3
SSB1-45	Canadian Animals Gr. 1-2
SSJ1-37	Canadian Arctic Inuit Gr. 2-3
SSJ1-53	Canadian Black History Gr. 4-8
SSJ1-57	Canadian Comprehension Gr. 1-2
SSJ1-58	Canadian Comprehension Gr. 3-4
SSJ1-59	Canadian Comprehension Gr. 5-6
SSJ1-46	Canadian Industries Gr. 4-6
SSK1-12	Canadian Problem Solving Gr. 4-6
SSJ1-38	Canadian Provinces & Terr. Gr. 4-6
SSY1-07	Capitalization & Punctuation Gr. 1-3
SSN1-198	Captain Courageous NS Gr. 7-8
SSK1-11	Cars Problem Solving Gr. 3-4
SSN1-154	Castle in the Attic NS Gr. 4-6
SSF1-31	Castles & Kings Gr. 4-6
SSN1-144	Cat Ate My Gymsuit NS Gr. 4-6
SSPC-38	Cats B/W Pictures
SSB1-50	Cats – Domestic & Wild Gr. 4-6
SSN1-34	Cats in Literature Gr. 3-6
SSN1-212	Cay NS Gr. 7-8
SSM1-09	Celebrate Autumn Gr. 4-6
SSC1-39	Celebrate Christmas Gr. 4-6
SSC1-31	Celebrate Easter Gr. 4-6
SSC1-23	Celebrate Shamrock Day Gr. 2
SSM1-11	Celebrate Spring Gr. 4-6
SSC1-13	Celebrate Thanksgiving R. 3-4
SSM1-06	Celebrate Winter Gr. 4-6
SSB1-107	Cells, Tissues & Organs Gr. 7-8
SSB1-101	Characteristics of Flight Gr. 4-6
SSN1-66	Charlie & Chocolate Factory NS 4-6
SSN1-23	Charlotte's Web NS Gr. 4-6
SSB1-37	Chicks N'Ducks Gr. 2-4
SSA1-09	China Today Gr. 5-8
SSN1-70	Chocolate Fever NS Gr. 4-6
SSN1-241	Chocolate Touch NS Gr. 4-6
SSC1-38	Christmas Around the World Gr. 4-6
SSPC-42	Christmas B/W Pictures
SST1-08A	Christmas Gr. JK/SK
SST1-08B	Christmas Gr. 1
SST1-08C	Christmas Gr. 2-3
SSC1-04	Christmas Magic Gr. 1
SSC1-03	Christmas Tales Gr. 2-3
SSG1-06	Cinematography Gr. 5-8
SSPC-13	Circus B/W Pictures

Code #	Title and Grade
SSF1-03	Circus Magic Gr. 3-4
SSJ1-52	Citizenship/Immigration Gr. 4-8
SSN1-104	Classical Poetry Gr. 7-12
SSN1-227	Color Gr. 1-3
SSN1-203	Colour Gr. 1-3
SSN1-135	Come Back Amelia Bedelia NS 1-3
SSH1-11	Community Helpers Gr. 1-3
SSK1-02	Concept Cards & Activities Gr. P-1
SSN1-183	Copper Sunrise NS Gr. 7-8
SSN1-86	Corduroy & Pocket Corduroy NS 1-3
SSN1-124	Could Dracula Live in Wood NS 4-6
SSN1-148	Cowboy's Don't Cry NS Gr. 7-8
SSR1-01	Creativity with Food Gr. 4-8
SSB1-34	Creatures of the Sea Gr. 2-4
SSN1-208	Curse of the Viking Grave NS 7-8
SSN1-134	Danny Champion of World NS 4-6
SSN1-98	Danny's Run NS Gr. 7-8
SSK1-21	Data Management Gr. 4-6
SSB1-53	Dealing with Dinosaurs Gr. 4-6
SSN1-178	Dear Mr. Henshaw NS Gr. 4-6
SSB1-22	Deer Gr. 3-5
SSPC-20	Desert B/W Pictures
SSJ1-40	Development of Western Canada Gr. 7-8
SSA1-16	Development of Manufacturing 7-9
SSN1-105	Dicken's Christmas NS Gr. 7-8
SSN1-62	Different Dragons NS Gr. 4-6
SSPC-21	Dinosaurs B/W Pictures
SSB1-16	Dinosaurs Gr. 1
SST1-02A	Dinosaurs Gr. JK/SK
SST1-02B	Dinosaurs Gr. 1
SST1-02C	Dinosaurs Gr. 2-3
SSN1-175	Dinosaurs in Literature Gr. 1-3
SSJ1-26	Discover Nova Scotia Gr. 5-7
SSJ1-36	Discover Nunavut Territory Gr. 5-7
SSJ1-25	Discover Ontario Gr. 5-7
SSJ1-24	Discover PEI Gr. 5-7
SSJ1-22	Discover Québec Gr. 5-7
SSL1-01	Discovering the Library Gr. 2-3
SSB1-106	Diversity of Living Things Gr. 4-6
SSK1-27	Division Drills Gr. 4-6
SSB1-30	Dogs – Wild & Tame Gr. 4-6
SSPC-31	Dogs B/W Pictures
SSN1-196	Dog's Don't Tell Jokes NS Gr. 4-6
SSN1-182	Door in the Wall NS Gr. 4-6
SSB1-87	Down by the Sea Gr. 1-3
SSN1-189	Dr. Jeckyll & Mr. Hyde NS Gr. 4-6
SSG1-07	Dragon Trivia Gr. P-8
SSN1-102	Dragon's Egg NS Gr. 4-6
SSN1-16	Dragons in Literature Gr. 3-6
SSC1-06	Early Christmas Gr. 3-5
SSB1-109	Earth's Crust Gr. 6-8
SSC1-21	Easter Adventures Gr. 3-4
SSC1-17	Easter Delights Gr. P-K
SSC1-19	Easter Surprises Gr. 1
SSPC-12	Egypt B/W Pictures
SSN1-255	Egypt Game NS Gr. 4-6
SSF1-28	Egyptians Today & Yesterday Gr. 2-3
SSJ1-49	Elections in Canada Gr. 4-8
SSB1-108	Electricity Gr. 4-6
SSN1-02	Elves & the Shoemaker NS Gr. 1-3
SSH1-14	Emotions Gr. P-2
SSB1-85	Energy Gr. 4-6
SSN1-108	English Language Gr. 10-12
SSN1-156	Enjoying Eric Wilson Series Gr. 5-7
SSB1-64	Environment Gr. 4-6
SSR1-12	ESL Teaching Ideas Gr. K-8
SSN1-258	Esperanza Rising NS Gr. 4-6
SSR1-22	Exercises in Grammar Gr. 6
SSR1-23	Exercises in Grammar Gr. 7
SSR1-24	Exercises in Grammar Gr. 8
SSF1-20	Exploration Gr. 4-6
SSF1-15	Explorers & Mapmakers of Canada 7-8
SSJ1-54	Exploring Canada Gr. 1-3
SSJ1-56	Exploring Canada Gr. 1-6
SSJ1-55	Exploring Canada Gr. 4-6
SSH1-20	Exploring My School and Community Gr. 1
SSPC-39	Fables B/W Pictures
SSN1-15	Fables Gr. 4-6
SSN1-04	Fairy Tale Magic Gr. 3-5
SSPC-11	Fairy Tales B/W Pictures
SSN1-11	Fairy Tales Gr. 1-2
SSN1-199	Family Under the Bridge NS 4-6
SSPC-41	Famous Canadians B/W Pictures
SSJ1-12	Famous Canadians Gr. 4-8
SSN1-210	Fantastic Mr. Fox NS Gr. 4-6
SSB1-36	Fantastic Plants Gr. 4-6
SSPC-04	Farm Animals B/W Pictures
SSB1-15	Farm Animals Gr. 1-2
SST1-03A	Farm Gr. JK/SK

Code #	Title and Grade
SST1-03B	Farm Gr. 1
SST1-03C	Farm Gr. 2-3
SSJ1-05	Farming Community Gr. 3-4
SSB1-44	Farmyard Friends Gr. P-K
SSJ1-45	Fathers of Confederation Gr. 4-8
SSB1-19	Feathered Friends Gr. 4-6
SST1-05A	February Gr. JK/SK
SST1-05B	February Gr. 1
SST1-05C	February Gr. 2-3
SSN1-03	Festival of Fairytales Gr. 3-5
SSC1-36	Festivals Around the World Gr. 2-3
SSN1-168	First 100 Sight Words Gr. 1
SSC1-32	First Days at School Gr. 1
SSJ1-06	Fishing Community Gr. 3-4
SSN1-170	Flowers for Algernon NS Gr. 7-8
SSN1-128	Fly Away Home NS Gr. 4-6
SSD1-05	Food: Fact, Fun & Fiction Gr. 1-3
SSD1-06	Food: Nutrition & Invention Gr. 4-6
SSB1-118	Force and Motion Gr. 1-3
SSB1-119	Force and Motion Gr. 4-6
SSB1-25	Foxes Gr. 3-5
SSN1-172	Freckle Juice NS Gr. 1-3
SSB1-43	Friendly Frogs Gr. 1
SSB1-89	Fruits & Seeds Gr. 4-6
SSN1-137	Fudge-a-Mania NS Gr. 4-6
SSB1-14	Fun on the Farm Gr. 3-4
SSR1-49	Fun with Phonics Gr. 1-3
SSPC-06	Garden Flowers B/W Pictures
SSK1-03	Geometric Shapes Gr. 2-5
SSC1-18	Get the Rabbit Habit Gr. 1-2
SSN1-209	Giver, The NS Gr. 7-8
SSN1-190	Go Jump in the Pool NS Gr. 4-6
SSG1-03	Goal Setting Gr. 6-8
SSG1-08	Gr. 3 Test – Parent Guide
SSG1-99	Gr. 3 Test – Teacher Guide
SSG1-09	Gr. 6 Language Test – Parent Guide
SSG1-97	Gr. 6 Language Test – Teacher Guide
SSG1-10	Gr. 6 Math Test – Parent Guide
SSG1-96	Gr. 6 Math Test – Teacher Guide
SSG1-98	Gr. 6 Math/Lang. Test – Teacher Guide
SSK1-14	Graph for all Seasons Gr. 1-3
SSN1-117	Great Brain NS Gr. 4-6
SSN1-90	Great Expectations NS Gr. 7-8
SSN1-169	Great Gilly Hopkins NS Gr. 4-6
SSN1-197	Great Science Fair Disaster NS 4-6
SSN1-138	Greek Mythology Gr. 7-8
SSN1-113	Green Gables Detectives NS 4-6
SSC1-26	Groundhog Celebration Gr. 2
SSC1-25	Groundhog Day Gr. 1
SSB1-113	Growth & Change in Animals Gr. 2-3
SSB1-114	Growth & Change in Plants Gr. 2-3
SSB1-48	Guinea Pigs & Friends Gr. 3-5
SSB1-104	Habitats Gr. 4-6
SSPC-18	Halloween B/W Pictures
SST1-04A	Halloween Gr. JK/SK
SST1-04B	Halloween Gr. 1
SST1-04C	Halloween Gr. 2-3
SSC1-10	Halloween Gr. 4-6
SSC1-08	Halloween Happiness Gr. 1
SSC1-29	Halloween Spirits Gr. P-K
SSC1-42	Happy Valentines Day Gr. 3
SSN1-205	Harper Moon NS Gr. 7-8
SSN1-123	Harriet the Spy NS Gr. 4-6
SSC1-11	Harvest Time Wonders Gr. 1
SSN1-136	Hatchet NS Gr. 7-8
SSC1-09	Haunting Halloween Gr. 2-3
SSN1-91	Hawk & Stretch NS Gr. 4-6
SSC1-30	Hearts & Flowers Gr. P-K
SSN1-22	Heidi NS Gr. 4-6
SSN1-120	Help I'm Trapped in My NS 4-6
SSN1-24	Henry & the Clubhouse NS 4-6
SSN1-184	Hobbit NS Gr. 7-8
SSN1-122	Hoboken Chicken Emerg. NS 4-6
SSN1-250	Holes NS Gr. 4-6
SSN1-116	How Can a Frozen Detective NS 4-6
SSN1-89	How Can I be a Detective if I NS 4-6
SSN1-96	How Come the Best Clues... NS 4-6
SSN1-133	How To Eat Fried Worms NS 4-6
SSR1-48	How To Give a Presentation Gr. 4-6
SSN1-125	How To Teach Writing Through 7-9
SSR1-10	How To Write a Composition 6-10
SSR1-09	How To Write a Paragraph 5-10
SSR1-08	How To Write an Essay Gr. 7-12
SSR1-03	How To Write Poetry & Stories 4-6
SSD1-07	Human Body Gr. 2-4
SSD1-02	Human Body Gr. 4-6
SSN1-25	I Want to Go Home NS Gr. 4-6
SSH1-06	I'm Important Gr. 2-3
SSH1-07	I'm Unique Gr. 4-6

Publication Listing

Code #	Title and Grade	Code #	Title and Grade	Code #	Title and Grade	Code #	Title and Grade
SSN1-76	Wayside School is Falling Down NS 4-6						
SSB1-60	Weather Gr. 4-6						
SSN1-17	Wee Folk in Literature Gr. 3-5						
SSPC-08	Weeds B/W Pictures						
SSQ1-04	Welcome Back – Big Book Pkg 1-3						
SSB1-73	Whale Preservation Gr. 5-8						
SSH1-08	What is a Community? Gr. 2-4						
SSH1-01	What is a Family? Gr. 2-3						
SSH1-09	What is a School? Gr. 1-2						
SSJ1-32	What is Canada? Gr. P-K						
SSN1-79	What is RAD? Read and Discover 2-4						
SSB1-62	What is the Weather Today? Gr. 2-4						
SSN1-194	What's a Daring Detective NS 4-6						
SSH1-10	What's My Number Gr. P-K						
SSR1-02	What's the Scoop on Words Gr. 4-6						
SSN1-73	Where the Red Fern Grows NS 7-8						
SSN1-87	Where the Wild Things Are NS 1-3						
SSN1-187	Whipping Boy NS Gr. 4-6						
SSN1-226	Who is Frances Rain? NS Gr. 4-6						
SSN1-74	Who's Got Gertie & How...? NS 4-6						
SSN1-131	Why did the Underwear ... NS 4-6						
SSC1-28	Why Wear a Poppy? Gr. 2-3						
SSJ1-11	Wild Animals of Canada Gr. 2-3						
SSPC-07	Wild Flowers B/W Pictures						
SSB1-18	Winter Birds Gr. 2-3						
SSZ1-03	Winter Olympics Gr. 4-6						
SSM1-04	Winter Wonderland Gr. 1						
SSC1-01	Witches Gr. 3-4						
SSN1-213	Wolf Island NS Gr. 1-3						
SSE1-09	Wolfgang Amadeus Mozart 6-9						
SSB1-23	Wolves Gr. 3-5						
SSC1-20	Wonders of Easter Gr. 2						
SSB1-35	World of Horses Gr. 4-6						
SSB1-13	World of Pets Gr. 2-3						
SSF1-26	World War II Gr. 7-8						
SSN1-221	Wrinkle in Time NS Gr. 7-8						
SSPC-02	Zoo Animals B/W Pictures						
SSB1-08	Zoo Animals Gr. 1-2						
SSB1-09	Zoo Celebration Gr. 3-4						